BOOK 1

Let the Kids Do It!

A Manual for Self-Direction Through Indirect Guidance

Preschool Through Grade 3

Norma Ziegler
Betty Larson
Jane Byers

Fearon Teacher Aids, a division of DAVID S. LAKE PUBLISHERS
Belmont, California

Dedication

Our thanks and appreciation to our colleagues at San Antonio College, especially to Elizabeth Culbertson, who provided inspiration and support by fostering an atmosphere in which creative thinking is valued; to Joyce Gray, who encouraged our use of these ideas in the campus Child Development Center; to the children who tried out the ideas; and to our families, who tolerated our meetings, our late-night writing sessions, and our constant deadlines.

Norma Ziegler
Betty Larson
Jane Byers

Editor: *Kathleen Kraft*

Designer: *John Edeen*

Illustrator: *Betty Larson*

Edited and produced by The Hampton-Brown Company, Inc., Carmel, California

ISBN-0-8224-4275-2
Printed in the United States of America
1. 9 8 7 6

Contents

Why Use Indirect Guidance?

One of the goals of early childhood education is to help children become self-directive. If children can be assisted in thinking, discovering, and creating with only a limited amount of adult intervention, they will have an excellent start toward independent learning and living as adults.

THE PHILOSOPHY OF INDIRECT GUIDANCE

Indirect guidance fosters self-direction and independence in young children. As used in this book, the term "indirect guidance" refers to the philosophy of guidance in which the teacher or caregiver carefully structures the physical environment and plans activities to predispose desirable classroom behavior. As the teacher, you would not be as directly involved as when giving verbal directions or explanations nor as when leading or holding a child. Instead, you would use a number of specific guidance techniques and materials that encourage children to participate in the learning process by locating and using materials by themselves. As the teacher or caregiver, you are then free to interact with the children more effectively and creatively and to devote more time to guiding and teaching.

ESSENTIAL CONCEPTS

Basic concepts essential to the effective use of indirect guidance in early childhood education include the following:

- the classroom organization and arrangement
- the schedule of activities during each day
- the activities in the classroom and outdoors

Other concepts to consider when implementing indirect guidance include:

- the effective use of transitional activities to move smoothly from one activity to another
- the establishment of routines and limits
- the use of pictorial messages, such as drawings, commercial pictures, charts, and symbols

COMPARISON OF DIRECT AND INDIRECT GUIDANCE

For illustrative purposes, it is helpful to look at two classrooms, comparing the techniques of direct and indirect guidance.

In Classroom A, the children are totally dependent on the teacher for all direction, and the teacher is giving many verbal directions. This teacher is busily setting out materials for the waiting children. He or she is continually helping one child after another, while other children are waiting for assistance or asking for supplies. Some of the children finish their tasks early and begin to disturb others.

There is a great deal of waiting in this classroom. Children wait for materials and for assistance. Sometimes the children wait to ask if they can wash their hands or use the restroom. The children frequently find nonconstructive ways to fill this waiting time.

Classroom B is a self-directed situation using indirect guidance techniques. The children have been carefully introduced to the classroom and they are familiar with the routines and schedule. The children know that they can locate and use materials by themselves. The boys and girls in this classroom have learned that there are many sources of information and assistance in addition to the teacher. Cues or markers on the shelves remind them where to return materials. Charts and pictures offer ideas for the use of the materials. Picture cues also remind the children of the location of their cubbyholes or lockers and cots. A planning board assists the children in selecting activities and in moving from one activity or interest center to another. Child-sized brooms, buckets, and sponges are available so that children can take care of their spills or messes.

The children feel very much a part of this class. They are enjoying and contributing to the experience. Moreover, there are few opportunities and little reason for classroom disturbance.

The first example may present a stereotype of the harried and exhausted teacher. This teacher may feel that children in early childhood classes must be constantly directed or assisted with each and every task because they are "too little" or "not capable" of self-direction. The children quickly notice and often resist this attitude.

In contrast, the teacher in the second example has arranged the classroom and activities so that the children feel capable of self-direction. This teacher may find that there are times when directions are necessary. However, when verbal directions are limited in number, the children tend to pay more attention to them.

ADVANTAGES OF INDIRECT GUIDANCE TECHNIQUES

As a teacher in a self-directed classroom using indirect guidance techniques, you do not have to be a director or a supervisor. There is time to assist the children's growth in the areas of social, emotional, physical, and intellectual development. Some of your roles might include the following activities.

Observing and Evaluating the Children at Play

In a classroom of independent learners, you are freed from many of the time-consuming "housekeeping" chores. The children do them automatically as part of the self-directed class. This allows you more opportunity to observe and to gain insight into the interactions between the children and between the children and their environment. You have an opportunity to see situations from the children's point of view, gathering much more information as an observer than can be obtained in a more directive role. The outcome is more time and energy to work with those children who need remedial or enrichment types of activities or to select appropriate new or additional activities based on your observations.

Reflecting and Verbalizing on the Children's Actions

The role of reflector provides you with the opportunity to reflect or verbally describe children's actions. Their knowledge of behavior is strengthened by a vocabulary that meaningfully relates to the child's own experiences. You can express an interest in them that builds self-confidence and a sense of importance.

Expanding Play

You can expand the children's play by observing them during an activity time and offering ideas, materials, and information. In this type of interaction, children are free to accept or reject ideas within the limits of the classroom situation.

Serving as a Role Model

You can be a behavior model by entering a play situation as a player. This activity often raises the level of the children's participation and makes it more meaningful. As the teacher, you would not lead the play activity. Rather, you would add a new element or a new thought while permitting the children to be the leaders and to instigate the ideas.

HOW TO USE THIS BOOK

This book describes how to set up an early-childhood classroom which resembles the second classroom discussed in this introduction. Indirect guidance techniques are integral to the self-directed classroom. They are discussed from six basic points of view:

- classroom arrangement
- pictorial messages and materials
- schedules
- routines
- limits
- transitional activities

You will find references to pictorial messages (symbols and rebuses) throughout this book. These messages include markers, cues, pictorial recipes, and pictorial directions that are appropriate for use with young children. Additional rebus activities, patterns for drawings, and teaching suggestions for use with rebus charts are presented in the companion MAKEMASTER® book, entitled Book 2, *LET THE KIDS DO IT!: Symbols and Rebus Charts.*

This book is not intended to be a text of highly developed and researched theories. Rather, it is a workbook, or, better, a "createbook." It explains the rationale for using indirect guidance techniques to encourage self-direction in early-childhood classrooms. It also provides specific guidelines for implementing those techniques, tailoring them to your unique classroom situation.

The companion book provides reproducible blackline patterns for the materials discussed in this text. The blackline patterns are easy to trace or duplicate. Printed on perforated pages, the MAKEMASTER® patterns will save time and energy in producing the indirect guidance materials for your classroom.

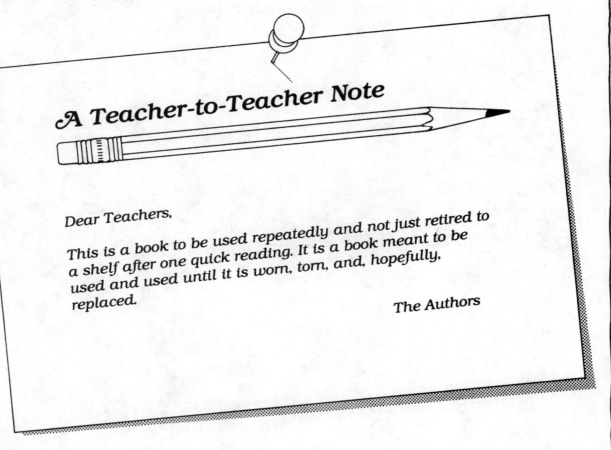

A Teacher-to-Teacher Note

Dear Teachers,

This is a book to be used repeatedly and not just retired to a shelf after one quick reading. It is a book meant to be used and used until it is worn, torn, and, hopefully, replaced.

The Authors

PART I

Indirect Guidance Through Classroom Organization

 Chapter 1
Classroom Arrangement

 Chapter 2
Planning Boards

 Chapter 3
Cuing the Classroom

 Chapter 4
Symbol Charts and Rebus Charts

 Chapter 5
Types of Interest Centers

1

Classroom Arrangement

Much indirect learning and many self-directed activities are stimulated by good classroom arrangement and the proper location of supplies and materials. The classroom arrangement will tend to determine the children's response and interactions. If the environment requires children to make choices, they will learn to make decisions. If the materials are placed according to cues, indicators, or outlines, the children will learn to put things in their place and will learn the skill of organization. The following suggestions will assist you in setting up a physical environment that will encourage self-direction and will provide a place for the indirect guidance activities that are suggested throughout this book.

SURVEY THE PHYSICAL PLANT

Your classroom can be arranged or rearranged to encourage self-direction and indirect guidance. Take into consideration the following factors:

- overall appearance of the room
- relationship between areas
- location of exits and entrances
- traffic flow or pattern of movement
- location of the water source and electrical outlets
- location and availability of storage places for children's toys and for teaching materials
- sources of natural and artificial light
- locations of restrooms and the kitchen
- space for eating and sleeping

PLAN THE LOCATION OF INTEREST CENTERS

Interest centers or learning centers are areas of the room that are designated for particular activities. The concept of interest centers is basic to the use of indirect guidance in the early childhood classroom. Young children appear to learn more thoroughly by doing, touching, feeling, handling, and interacting with materials and equipment. They also learn more readily from things they *choose* to do, rather than from things they are told or forced to do. Early childhood classes do not learn well from lectures or upon demand. The children have different attention spans. Well-planned interest centers and indirect guidance techniques permit children to play within the time and limits allowed, but in their own way.

Draw the Classroom to Scale

Drawing the general arrangement of the room to scale on graph paper will help you decide where interest centers can fit into your classroom. A sketch like this one can be drawn to fit the floor plan of any room. Locate the physical characteristics and traffic flow on the plan. Show tiled and carpeted floors, restrooms, and other important areas. Show the placement of permanent equipment and physical facilities, such as doors, windows, exits, entrances, restrooms, built-in storage, electric outlets, and water sources.

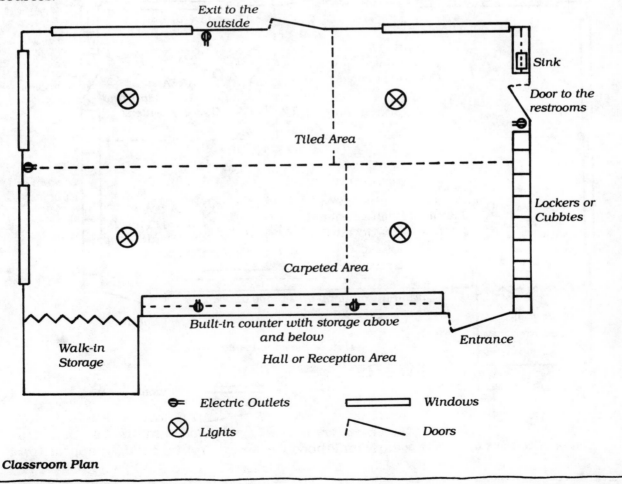

Classroom Plan

Divide the Classroom into Areas

If there is a carpeted area, designate it for the Block Center, Music Center, and group experiences. Art, Cooking, and Science Centers are more practical on a tiled area. Electricity is needed for Cooking, Music, and Discovery Centers. A source of water is necessary for Art, Water Play, Cooking, and Discovery Centers. A Table Game Center and an Art Center need tables and a bookcase.

The following block plan is for a simple rectangular room. Mark the major areas of the room on the plan according to the physical facilities, then locate the interest centers in the appropriate areas. Each classroom will offer its own challenges.

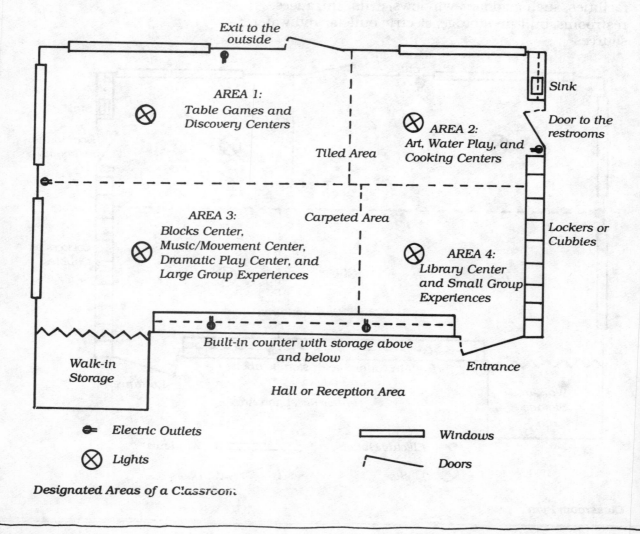

Designated Areas of a Classroom

In the classroom shown here, Area 1 is on the tiled floor and is near natural light. The Table Games and Discovery Centers could be located here, using bookcases and tables. Area 2 is near the water source. Art, Water Play, and Cooking Centers could be located here. The floor is tiled and windows provide natural light for the area. The outside exit makes it easy to move active centers like the Water Play Center and Art Center outdoors. It also makes it possible to move the outdoor workshop to the inside if necessary. A bookcase could easily divide this area from the adjacent area.

Area 3 is the largest area and accommodates large-group experiences and movement activities. It is carpeted, has a natural light source, and is out of the heavy-traffic area. The walk-in storage closet can store the blankets or cots which will be used in this area. The built-in cabinets can store materials for the Block Center and Dramatic Play Center. These centers function well in adjacent locations. If a piano is available, it could be used as a divider between areas 1 and 3. Kitchen-type play equipment, a block storage case, and screens could also be used as dividers between areas.

Area 4 is the smallest area and could provide a quiet corner for the library. It is near the entry door, giving the children an opportunity to make an easy transition from home to school and school to home. This kind of quiet area is a good place to greet the children and to calm them before they leave. You can gather a small group here for a story or talk time.

Select Appropriate Content for Interest Centers

After the room has been thoroughly examined and the overall plans made, it is time to consider what specific interest or learning centers you will use. Remember that not all centers will be available at all times. Some areas can serve two functions. For example, the Library Center may become a puppet theater. The selection of interest centers will indirectly determine what activities the children will engage in throughout the year. Interest centers might include the following:

- Art or Arts and Crafts
- Blocks or Construction
- Cooking (kitchen science or food preparation)
- Discovery (math/science or nature)
- Dramatic Play (family living, homemaking, or housekeeping)
- Library or Listening; Language or Story
- Music/Motor/Movement
- Table Games (manipulative materials, math, or readiness)
- Water Play or Sand/Mud
- Workshop (woodworking or crafts)
- Rotating Center (This center will change focus according to the current interests of the children or the topics being considered.)

The content and name of a center will depend on the teacher, the school, and the children. In recent years, name changes have occurred which seem logical. For example, as more and more creativity has been stressed in art, the crafts have been moved into the Arts Center. The term *woodworking* has been changed to *workshop* as more diversified activities have occurred there. As the importance of creative thought has been emphasized, the activities that occur in the kitchen-housekeeping area have expanded to include many other situations. These changes have resulted in the name dramatic play for the homemaking-family living center. The former *science corner* with its plants, aquarium, and rock collection has been replaced by an area where many cognitive concepts are stressed. The newest name for this area is *discovery*. When the names of centers were placed on center markers, and when children began to use the vocabulary of the centers in their language, the names were changed to those which the children could say. For example, the Manipulative Center became the Table Game Center because it was easier for very young children to say.

Determine the Location of Each Interest Center

As the teacher, you will decide the types and locations of the centers. They must fit the needs of the children and the physical facilities available. Your consideration of the situation might include the following specific factors:

- age of children
- location of noisy centers near other noisy centers (For example, give the Blocks Center and Music Center adjacent locations.)
- location of quiet centers near other quiet centers (For example, give the Library Center and the Science Center adjacent locations.)
- location of centers near one another to facilitate interaction (For example, locate the Blocks Center near the Dramatic Play center.)
- storage space for items that are currently not being used
- adequate space for individual centers (Music/Movement and Blocks Centers require generous space, while the Library and Table Games Centers do not demand as much.)
- quantities, types, and sizes of available or potential equipment, furnishings, and materials
- space for displaying materials to encourage self-direction
- a large open area for large-group experiences and several small open areas for small-group experiences
- places and spaces to display finished products, to save items, or to set aside things to work on later

A great deal of thinking and consideration are necessary to plan the location and activities for each interest center. Chapter 5 offers guidelines for the physical arrangement of each suggested center. The physical arrangement of the center, together with the suggested rebus charts and other activities, will indirectly guide the children who use the center. The companion MAKEMASTER® book offers teaching suggestions for seven interest centers and for classroom routines, as well as a number of patterns for symbols to indirectly guide the children.

Part of the interest-center concept is to encourage decision-making on the part of the children. The planning board offers a means of helping the children commit to a specific center. Each child has a nametag that is designed to be hung on a hook for the interest center he or she selects. The children signify their interest-center selection by their placement of the nametags. The number of children at each interest center is determined by the number of hooks on the interest-center planning board. Chapter 2 discusses the concept and use of individual and central planning boards as part of indirect guidance in the early childhood classroom.

A Teacher-to-Teacher Note

Dear Teachers,

The classroom arrangement is a much more effective guidance technique than are direct guidance methods. With a well-planned learning environment, the need for direct intervention will be minimal. You and the children will enjoy the learning process.

The Authors

Planning Boards

The *planning board* is a relatively new indirect guidance technique. Other names for this planning device are *choosing boards* or *activity boards*. The concept is designed to encourage decision-making and to help children to understand the relationships between the parts of the program. The children learn self-direction and independent interaction in an informal manner.

The children use the planning boards to signify their choice of an interest center by hanging their nametags on one of the hooks or spaces on the interest-center planning board. Therefore, the nametags are part of the planning board technique and provide a concrete affirmation of each child's decision and plan for the time span.

Each child has a nametag made from poster board, fiberboard, or a plastic or metal jar lid. Each nametag has a hole so that it will hang on a planning board hook. You can use the nametags to indicate various groupings if the nametags are different colors and shapes.

One side of the nametag will have the child's first name neatly printed along with a symbol that has been identified as that child's special indicator. The symbol might be a sticker, a picture, or a colored shape. Each child should have a different symbol. If possible, make the name of the symbol begin with the same letter as the child's name. The symbol is also used on the child's cot and locker or cubbyhole. Print the child's first and last name on the reverse side of the nametag using manuscript printing.

Children's nametags show their names and are cued with shapes and symbols.

The planning board concept can take one of two basic forms. The first idea involves the use of *individual* boards that are located in each of the interest centers in the classroom. The second concept is more advanced and involves the use of a single, *central* planning board which represents the entire array of interest centers. Each individual interest center is represented on the single board. It is important that the children understand the individual boards before introducing the central planning board.

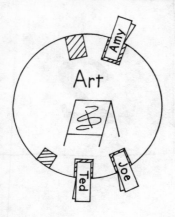

**Individual
Planning Board**

THE INDIVIDUAL PLANNING BOARD

Place individual planning boards at each interest center in the classroom. The board contains a picture of the activity for that center, the name of the center printed in manuscript printing, and an indication of the number of children who may play in that center at any one time. This indication may be several hooks for nametags or several pockets in which a child may place the nametag.

THE CENTRAL PLANNING BOARD

When the children understand the use of the individual planning boards, a central planning board can be introduced. This coincides with the development of the children: individual parts of a complex situation are understood first.

The central planning board may look something like the illustration on page 17.

You may be able to use existing furnishings to make the central planning board. Consider using the back of a bookcase which has pegboard as the backing material, or use a pegboard-type movable screen, a bulletin board, or a solid-backed cabinet. When a pegboard is used, the pegboard hooks can indicate the number of children who may be in a center at one time. If you use a solid-backed board, the indicators must be pockets, screw-in hooks, or paste-on hooks.

Divide the central board into sections to correspond to the interest centers. Colored tape works well for this purpose. Place an interest-center marker in each section. This marker may be a photograph of the children playing in the particular center, a drawing that is representative of that center, or an appropriate picture cut from a supply catalog. Mount each marker on a rectangle of poster board, laminate it, or cover it with adhesive-backed transparent paper. Print the name of the center on the center marker. Color-cue the central planning board markers to the identification markers in the individual centers to assist the children in identifying the connection between the two.

Include enough "play spaces" in each interest center. There should be enough spaces so that each child has the opportunity to select a center. If each "play space" is represented by a hook, provide twice as many hooks as there are children.

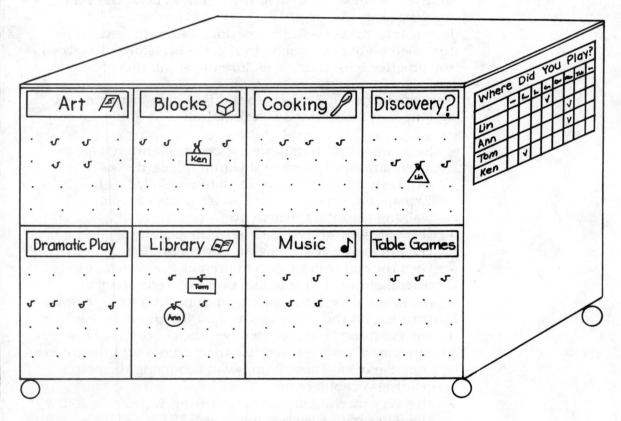

The back of a bookcase can be used as a central planning board area. Mount a "Where Did You Play?" chart at the side and add a page for each week of school.

HOW TO INTRODUCE THE CONCEPT

Work with a group of five or six children when you are beginning to use the planning board concept. Tell them about activities that will occur in the centers and any other necessary facts regarding the play. If necessary, go with them to the centers and point out the arrangements for the day. Each child can choose the interest center where she or he will play by placing a nametag on the center's planning board hooks.

Work with one group of children at a time until all of the children have been introduced to the planning board. When each child understands the system, two groups can be combined. Eventually 15 or 20 children can plan and evaluate together. Explanations must be kept short, and all the children need to have an opportunity to participate. Spend individual time with the children who don't seem to understand in order to help them comprehend the concepts.

It may take some use and experimentation to learn to use this method of helping children make decisions. It is worth the practice to encourage children to think independently.

Here are some suggestions that might help introduce the system of self-direction to the children.

- Start with individual interest-center planning boards. Then advance to a central planning board.
- Begin slowly and simply. Explain carefully but briefly.
- Explain the procedure to a small group of children by walking through the activity.
- Use only four or five centers in the beginning. Add more centers as the children gain understanding.
- Give the children time to figure out the system and to assimilate the information. Don't rush or push.
- Always include a symbolic representation to go with the printing on the nametags and on the center markers for the planning board. Remember, the children cannot read, but they will soon recognize their names and the interest-center names. These names will be among their first reading vocabulary.
- Use very careful manuscript printing. If possible, follow the letter patterns shown in the MAKEMASTER® book. Children reproduce what they see, and some of them may be ready to print their names and some simple words.
- Use genuine and sincere praise and encouragement as the children learn the procedure.
- Share the children's accomplishments with their parents.

HOW TO USE THE SYSTEM

Consider these suggestions for using the planning board concept. Several ideas are listed for each situation described.

When an interest center is closed:

- Remove the nametag hooks whenever possible.
- Print CLOSED on the back of the name card for the interest center. Turn it over, or make a center name card with an international slash to indicate "closed." This could be done on the back of the regular card.
- Remove all evidence of that center from the central board and put a "stop" or "closed" sign in the center. This works well for centers such as Water Play or the Workshop, which are available only part of the time.
- Print CLOSED on several cardboard circles. Put strings on them and hang them on the appropriate hooks.

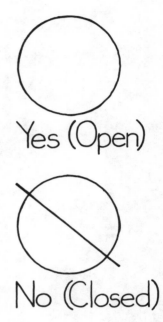

Yes (Open)

No (Closed)

When making central planning board cards to show the names of the interest centers:

- Color-cue the name card to the interest-center marker.
- Include a picture of the general activity for that center by using one of the following:
  1. Photographs of children playing at the center
  2. Pictures cut from supply catalogs and mounted on cards
  3. Sketches (stick figures are fine)
  4. Pictures from a magazine
- Plan a place to store central board cards so those removed can be readily available. A divided household caddy provides storage space for unused cards, nametags, and a pencil. Keep it near the central board.

When changing a center from one use or content area to another:

- Change the picture on the central planning board to correspond to the new use. For example, if the library is to be a puppet theater, remove the Library Center card and put up a planning board card picturing a puppet theater. Children learn that one area can serve several functions. As the children become accustomed to the changes, it may not be necessary to change the card. The children can make the change in their minds.

When an interest center is fully occupied:

- Some children will object, some will accept, and some will try to do something about the situation. They might try to place one name on top of another, move a name and replace it with their own, add a hook by taking it from another place, cry, or verbally object.
- Explain that if an interest center is full, a child may not play there until someone moves. Be firm but friendly about enforcing this. Delayed gratification is hard to learn, but children need to know they can't always have *what* they want *when* they want it.
- Teach the children to negotiate. Help them work out a solution. Ask the children how long they think they should play in a center before they have to move. Help them reach a solution. Be prepared to serve as an arbitrator and to remind them. Do not make the decision for the children.

When a child plays in the same center all the time:

- Rotate the order of choosing so that the interest center is full when it is that child's turn to choose.
- Provide more interesting activities in the other centers and encourage the children to try them.
- If there is no demand for the interest center, permit the child to play there. He or she apparently has a need that the center is filling.
- Occasionally you may say, "All month you have chosen where you want to play. Today it is my turn to choose." If the activities planned are interesting, most children will not object. Be sure they have an opportunity to switch after a short while if they choose to do so.

When a child "jumps" from center to center and finds it difficult to stay with anything:

- Set a short time limit which is a *minimum* time. Let the children help decide this time. The children *may change* at the end of the time period but are *not required to*.
- Give praise and encouragement for appropriate play. This is an extremely effective way to get children to change behavior or to continue acceptable behavior.
- Be sure the activities are interesting and neither too difficult nor too easy.

When a child doesn't understand the interest-center procedure:

- Use individual teaching. Work with the individual child for awhile, helping the child to make a choice, play in a center, and change to another center.
- Let the child choose first and help the child make a decision. Be available to assist when a change is indicated.
- Observe this child. Additional evaluation of the child might be indicated, especially if the child does not understand the concept after several weeks of individual teaching.

HOW TO ENCOURAGE PLANNING AND EVALUATION

Plan to meet with the children for a planning and an evaluation time each day. During the planning time, the children discuss the activities in the centers and what they will do. The evaluation time may be held at the end of the interest-center time. When evaluating, encourage the children to discuss where they have played and what they have done. You will then evaluate the activities of the day.

Using a planning board helps children to:

- make choices
- stay with their choices and follow through on their actions
- share and take turns
- experience delayed gratification by sometimes having to wait for an area
- negotiate and arbitrate
- evaluate by talking about where they played and what they did

Children who use a planning board learn to *plan*, *participate*, and *evaluate* their actions. They go through all the steps involved in the learning process and lay the foundation for future learning. The use of the planning board encourages much self-direction and independent learning.

3

Cuing
the Classroom

A cue is a secondary stimulus that guides behavior. In the early childhood classroom, a cue is a hint, a reminder, or an indicator. When color or picture cues are used with young children, the goal is to guide their behavior with little or no verbal instruction. It is always necessary to remember that few children can read, and those who do read are only beginning to recognize words.

However, if children become accustomed to seeing and using cues, they will develop a respect for organization and equipment. Young children are able to use cues to find and use things with minimal adult assistance. Self-learning occurs. Teachers are freed from giving constant reminders about where things are located and how to use them. More time is available to interact in positive ways with the children in true learning situations.

Many cues are used in an early childhood classroom that emphasizes self-direction and indirect guidance. All the MAKEMASTER® patterns in the companion book are variations of cues. These cues are used in the following ways:

- Interest-center markers
- Shelf indicators
- Music cues
- Cuing picture files and music files
- Helping Charts
- Planning Boards
- Symbol Charts
- Rebus Charts
- Rebus Stories

This chapter offers suggestions for making and using some of these cues in the early childhood classroom. Rebus charts, picture files and music files, and rebus stories are discussed in Book 2.

CENTER MARKERS

Center markers are pictorial "signs." They are cues or indicators that show the activity that will occur in an interest center or an area of the room or playground. Using interest-center markers in individual centers provides the children with a clue as to the activity in which they will be involved if they choose to go to that center. The adults also understand the center's function at a glance.

In the beginning, it is suggested that you use only four or five center markers to correspond to the first interest centers you introduce to the children. It is advisable to color-cue the interest-center markers to the planning board indicators so the children can relate their planning board selection to the center in which they are going to play. (Refer to Chapter 2, Planning Boards.) Mark interest centers with any of the following:

- a sign
- a poster
- a mobile
- a wall hanging
- a dropped ceiling

Signs cue each interest center. If a second language is used in school, label the signs in both languages.

Signs and Posters

Signs can be simple, but they must be clear. Include a drawing or picture that represents the center's activity and write the name of the center in manuscript printing. If a second language is prevalent in the school's neighborhood, it might be advisable to include a label in that language too. The children will associate the activities of the center with the drawing or picture and the corresponding words.

A poster is generally more complex than a sign. It may be larger and include more detail. A poster would include the name of the interest center, and it would show pictures or drawings of activities in that center. You can use photographs of the children playing in the center. Actual objects used in the center will make the poster three-dimensional. For example, a puppet or a flannel-board figure could be included on the Library Center poster. A rock or a shell could add interest to the Discovery Center poster, and doll house furniture could be included in the Dramatic Play Center poster. You can include a label in a second language if applicable.

Posters can contain three-dimensional objects used in the center.

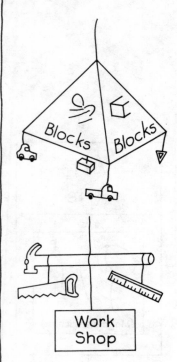

Mobiles can be constructed from a variety of materials.

Music Center Wall Hanging

Children can illustrate the wall hangings used as cues for interest centers.

Mobiles

Mobiles are an excellent way to mark interest centers and to indicate the other activity centers. Mobiles are interesting and fun for the children. To avoid a cluttered look and overstimulation of the children, mobiles should have a simple design and mark only a few interest centers.

Use a mobile to mark those interest centers that are available only part of the time. When the mobile is hung, it will announce that the center is open. For example, a cooking mobile might be hung on days when a cooking activity is scheduled. The water play mobile might be hung near the door when the water table will be available, or a mobile depicting a trip might be hung on a day when a study trip is planned.

The following suggestions and illustrations offer some ideas.

- Keep mobiles simple.
- Construct them carefully.
- Use well-executed manuscript printing.
- Children should be able to view the illustrations or objects from all sides and the bottom.
- Hang the mobiles low so the children can view them easily.
- Rotate various mobile designs to maintain interest.

Two sample mobiles to use as center markers are shown here. They are based on ideas from *Just Hanging Around* by Sue Bohlen, Joyce Digby, and Betty Larson, published by T. S. Denison and Co., Inc., Minneapolis, Minn. 1979.

Wall Hangings

Interest centers can be marked with wall hangings made by the children. To make a wall hanging, hem the top and bottom of a piece of burlap or other fabric and thread a dowel through the hems. Fasten a cord to hang the fabric from the wall. You can attach objects or drawings to the fabric with staples or stitches. The children can make an interest-center mural from an old sheet. Put the sheet on a table and provide the children with non-toxic felt-tip markers. Ask them to draw pictures of the activities in the interest center. You might want to go over the drawings with a permanent marker so that it can be washed. Children should not use permanent markers because they are toxic.

Canopies and Dropped Ceilings

A tent-like structure or a canopy can be made to enclose the library or dramatic play area. Suspend fabric squares or strips of fabric on dowels hung from the ceiling to form an enclosure. Then add a sign and pictures to indicate the name of the center, as shown by the illustration.

Children's artwork may provide another type of ceiling cue. Mount the artwork on cardboard. At about five years of age, children enter the realistic stage of painting or drawing. Ask a five-year-old to draw a picture of an interest center, for example, the Block Center. Then punch holes in all four corners of the drawing and suspend it from the ceiling. If holes are punched in two corners, the artwork can be used as a wall hanging. Add the name of the center to make an appropriate center marker.

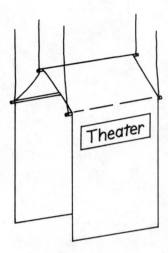

"Canopy" Ceiling

You can make an interesting dropped ceiling "sky" from an old blue sheet or a piece of blue fabric. Pin cutouts of planets, sun, and stars to the fabric and suspend it from string tied to all four corners.

SHELF INDICATORS

Shelf indicators are cues on shelves or other storage places that show children where items belong. They serve as reminders to children and to adults in the classroom. Everything has a place. Everything can easily be returned to its place if that place is easy to locate. For example, the outlines of a fire engine and a dump truck can be drawn on shelf paper and tacked down on a low shelf. These picture cues remind the children to return the toys to that shelf. What you cue and how you do it will depend on your classroom.

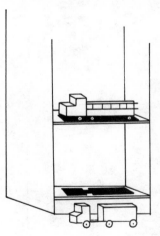

Shelf cues help children learn responsibility.

General Guidelines

Mark storage spaces in only one or two areas of the classroom at a time. Let the children become accustomed to the idea so that they do not become confused.

Start by marking the storage places for only a few items in an area. Point them out and show the children the cues. Make sure they understand the cues and use them to return the objects to the shelves. As more items are added, cue them. When items are rotated, change the cues.

Include printed words on the cues to encourage association between the printed words and the objects the words represent. This is the basis for reading. Many children will learn these words as their first reading vocabulary. Print in manuscript printing.

Draw the cues and print the words before placing the markers on the shelves. It is difficult to draw or write at an angle or on a rough surface. If individual cues are used, laminate them or cover them with adhesive-backed transparent vinyl so they will last longer.

Draw picture cues in pencil and then go over them with marking pen. This process will avoid marking the items being cued. It will also result in fewer mistakes and a more accurate representation of the object to be stored there.

When you are sure that the cues will be permanent, and *only* when you are sure, use oil-base markers. *Marks from these permanent markers are almost impossible to remove.* Therefore, use them for disposable items and items that get wet, such as meat trays that are used for water mixing. The marks won't smear, and the meat trays are easily replaced. You might use the permanent markers for cuing individual boxes or trays used for wet art projects.

Allow one child at a time to help cue a shelf. The child will feel very important, and he or she can teach the other children where things belong. Try to choose a child who frequently does not put things away. It may help develop organizational skills.

Types of Shelf Indicators

Several kinds of cuing methods can be used on shelves. Each teacher will have favorite ways to indicate where things belong, depending on a particular classroom and the children involved. These ideas are presented to help you begin the cuing process.

Outlines as Cues.   Draw the cues as simple outlines on paper and use it to line the shelves. This type of cuing works particularly well in a Table Game Center where the toys are changed frequently. If the paper is doubled, it will lay flat and can be turned over and used again.

Trays, box lids, rectangular baking pans, or plastic refrigerator containers may be used to store individual projects. Draw the outlines of objects that will be stored directly on the tray or on liners that are cut to fit in the tray. This system works well in the Art Center and in the Discovery Center, where individual projects lend themselves to being stored and rotated on the trays. For example, all the items for a "Float-or-Sink" activity (Book 2, pages 91-94) can be used and stored on a tray. Since these items frequently get wet, use a permanent marking pen and laminate or cover the cue with clear vinyl.

Cued Tray

Cues or outlines can be drawn on a large piece of butcher paper to encourage children to hang items on a pegboard. Draw the outlines of objects on the paper before attaching it to the back of a pegboard cabinet, screen, or bulletin board. It is important that the outlines match the location of pegboard hooks or cup hooks. The hooks must be placed very carefully to ensure correct alignment with the items that will hang there.

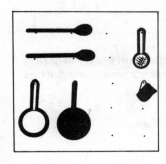

Cued Pegboard

Trays and shelves can be cued with simple outlines.

Illustrations as Cues. Actual toys or equipment can be illustrated on heavy cardboard. Cut out the pictures, laminate them, or cover them with clear vinyl. Fasten them securely to the shelf or to the rise of the shelf. This method works particularly well for unit blocks. For the younger children, the cues should be the exact size of the blocks or other objects. Place them on the floor of the shelves, so the blocks or other objects can be stored directly on top of them. Everything will be on one level. For older children, the cues may be made smaller and may be representative of the objects. Outlines may be placed on the rise of the shelf. The Block rebus chart in Book 2 shows children how to use the cues.

Codes as Cues. Colored dots can be used as cues to indicate the correct placement of objects. For example, a dot on a shelf can indicate the placement of each truck in a series of trucks or each instrument in a rhythm band. The child learns that one item belongs behind each dot.

Symbols and Size Relationships as Cues. A large rectangle on the front of a shelf might indicate the placement of large books; a smaller rectangle the place for smaller books; and a very small rectangle the place for the smallest books. The symbols that represent the books may be smaller than the actual books. For example, they could be one inch square, 2" x 3", and 5" x 7". Emphasize the size-relationship words *big, bigger,* and *biggest,* particularly with the older children.

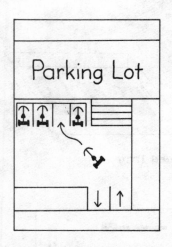

A diagram shows where tricycles should be parked.

Cue simple songs with simple songbooks of colored dots keyed to piano keys. Include song lyrics for prereading skills.

Cuing with Diagrams. General diagrams can be used with the older children to represent an area of the classroom. This type of exercise is the beginning of teaching children to read charts and graphs. You can use a cot chart, a diagram of easel locations, a chart that shows how to park tricycles in the parking lot, a diagram for an obstacle course, or a chart that shows the placement of children at tables. These diagrams are placed so that the children can easily see them. Spend some time explaining them to individual children who seem to be ready for the concept. If they do not understand, do not push the subject. Children who understand will frequently teach other children.

The preceding ideas for shelf indicators are offered as suggestions. In each program there will be individual activities that will indicate interesting cue ideas. The location of almost any item in the room can be indicated or cued for the children. These indicators will help their independent learning and self direction.

MUSIC CUES

Cuing can be used as a teaching aid. For example, children can learn to use the tape recorder and play the piano through cuing. Children often want to play the piano. A color can be assigned to each note. Colored dots may be placed on the white keys on the piano to cue some simple songs, such as "Mary Had a Little Lamb," "Happy Birthday," or "London Bridge." The tone bells, the xylophone, and the xylopipes may be cued in a similar way. If these song cues are placed on a strip of poster board that is approximately 36" long and 8" high and placed on a music holder, the children can see several measures of a song at a time and play the song by themselves. One line on a page is more satisfactory than a top-to-bottom sequence. The children cannot look from the keyboard to the music and keep their place.

The children want to use tape recorders and record players. Cue the "on" buttons with a green piece of tape and the "off" buttons with a red piece of tape. Mark the direction of use, with an arrow. Meet with small groups of children to talk about how to use these expensive pieces of equipment. Gather a box of records and tapes that the children can use. "Teacher only" records and tapes can be kept on a high storage shelf. With a few reminders, the children are able to use both the tape recorder and the record player without assistance.

Symbol Charts and Rebus Charts

4

Young children have difficulty listening to long explanations and understanding detailed instructions. They respond to short, concise, and easily understood directions and to visual cues. Young children seem to learn more completely by seeing pictures, illustrations, and symbols. By associating words with symbolic representations and pictorial messages, children lay a foundation for reading skills.

BASIC ACTION SYMBOLS

When you are working with young children, it is best to introduce pictorial messages with basic symbols that represent actions the children do every day. For example, the symbol of the eye indicates *see, look, observe* or *notice.* The symbol of the ear tells them to *listen* or *hear.* The symbol of the mouth represents *speaking, talking* or *responding,* and the tongue is the symbol for *taste.* Hands indicate *touching, feeling* or *doing.* The question mark represents *thinking, questioning* or *wondering.*

Touching

The symbols shown here are examples of those included as MAKEMASTER® patterns in Book 2. Use these patterns as cues to indicate appropriate actions to the children.

A slash through a symbol tells the chidren *not* to do an action. For example, a mouth with a slash line tells the children "do not talk." The use of the slash brings the new international slash into the classroom. The children see it as they travel on streets and highways. The slash can be used in other ways in the classroom. A set of traffic signs including "No U-Turn" and "No Walking" can be made for the tricycle area outdoors. A slash over the interest-center marker shows that the center is closed.

No Touching

HOW TO INTRODUCE ACTION SYMBOLS

- Make a set of the symbols on small cards and carry them in a pocket. Use them to indicate the action to the child when words are not appropriate or necessary.
- Add a symbol to a project you want the children to particularly notice or to do. For example, a large question mark displayed next to a science experiment will arouse the children's interest.
- Add an eye and question symbol to the beginning of rebus charts. They will indicate that the children are to look and think before they do what the rebus says. This chapter will give you instructions for making display devices.
- Print the words that correspond to the symbol. Point them out to the children. Use manuscript printing.
- If a second language is understood or used by the children, print the appropriate words in that language next to the symbol.
- When the children recognize the action symbol and the representative word, add another word for the action along with the name of the object. For example, the picture of a hand could have the word *touch* on it. Later, the words *do* or *feel* could be substituted. Still later, the word *hand* could be added. These words can teach that one symbol may represent more than one idea.
- Use these action symbols early in the year. They will simplify the transition to more complex pictorial representations such as the rebus charts and recipes.

HOW TO USE SYMBOL CHARTS

Introduce the symbol chart with a symbol story. Use two or three symbols together on one chart. The chart might say "look," "think," and "do." Print the words with the symbols. (Add the second-language words too, if that is a need in your area.)

The symbol charts can be used to gain attention and interest, to emphasize a point, to remind the children to do or not to do something, and to indicate a sequence or order. All of these things can be done nonverbally, or words can be added to make the technique both auditory and visual for the beginning reader.

Look-Think-Do Chart

A symbol chart reminds the children of actions and sequence.

Another symbolic representation that might be included on a chart is the use of *same* and *different*. The vocabulary for "same," "not the same," and "different" must be introduced to the children in a purposeful way through repetition over a time span. Same/different is a basic concept and is necessary for the understanding of all matching and classification tasks. Draw or show pictures of two like items to indicate sameness and two unlike items to indicate differences.

A "checking" activity is a more advanced use of symbols in the class. The children try to predict what will happen in a given situation and check their prediction to see if they are correct. Symbols can be used to represent the different steps in the situation. The example illustrated is a magnetic/non-magnetic science project. The sequence should move from left to right. Construct the magnetic/non-magnetic rebus chart (1) and place it in the Discovery Center. A box of objects (2), a checking tray with a question mark to indicate "to wonder" (3), a magnet (4), and an answer tray (5) are placed on the table. The child takes an object from the object box and predicts whether it is magnetic or not. He or she checks the prediction by using a magnet with the object and places the object in the proper answer box.

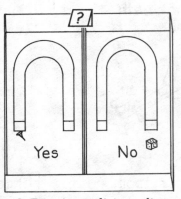

1. Rebus chart

 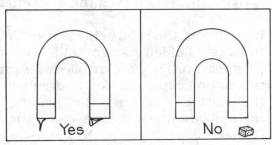 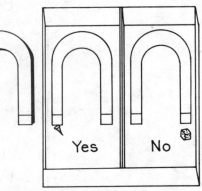

2. Box of objects   3. Tray to predict results   4. Magnet   5. Answer tray for results

Children predict an outcome, check the prediction, and place objects in the appropriate boxes.

DESCRIPTION OF A REBUS CHART

Rebus charts are basically picture stories or messages. For example, pictures can be substituted for words in stories, recipes, directions for activities, or instructions for use of equipment. Some activity-related rebuses are illustrated in this book.

Rebus charts are used to the best advantage in the classroom if they are introduced after the symbol charts have been used and understood by the children. Of course, children can be taught to understand rebus charts without previous exposure to the more simple form. However, the learning process is quicker and possibly more complete if the sequence is from easy to difficult.

There are several advantages to using rebus charts with young children. First, the charts encourage independence on the part of the children by providing *some* guidance for activities, but not requiring the *direct* intervention of the teacher. Second, the charts allow children to proceed with activities at their own pace, rather than being "herded along" with other children in a group situation. If a child needs to retrace a process or redo a step, it may be repeated until the child is *fully satisfied* with the outcome of the activity or has achieved the *mastery* level of learning.

In addition, the rebus charts provide additional experience in the skill of left-to-right and top-to-bottom reading progression. They are excellent for providing *successful* prereading experiences. Children will say they are "reading" the chart. Even though the "reading" is based upon memorization and picture clues, the children feel the thrill of making sense out of the letters and words on paper.

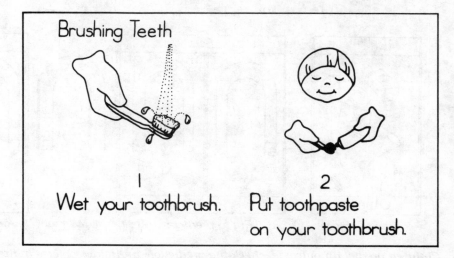

Rebus Chart

Rebus charts are fun for the children. The charts provide a puzzle or mystery-like situation to solve. This is apparent by the expressions on the children's faces as you introduce the chart sequence. They also provide an excellent experience in following a specific sequence or order of events to achieve a desired result. Finally, the rebus charts provide an opportunity to use memory skills in a valid situation.

HOW TO USE REBUS CHARTS

Begin with the most simple rebus charts. They will have less than four pictures. Consider introducing rebus charts with a single-step rebus such as the "Put on a smock" or the "Wash your hands" rebus. As the children become familiar with this one simple step, they are ready to move into the more complex charts. Gradually introduce the other rebus charts for familiar routines. Remember that the most simple rebus charts have less than four pictures. Be prepared for the children to repeat the routines over and over as they go through the process of familiarizing themselves with the directions on the chart. For a brief time, the rebus will be like a new toy and may elicit the same type of behavior response from the children.

After the rebuses for routines have been in use, you can introduce longer charts for recipes and activities. The rebuses which have fewer steps are easier for beginners to follow. Steps can be introduced one at a time if necessary. Later, you can introduce a rebus with several steps in a row. Although this may be a simple rebus, it introduces a new concept: to follow several steps in sequence all on one chart. Introduce each level of rebus chart slowly and give some explanation of the steps. When the children understand sequence, begin to use the rebuses with four and five steps and those which require left-to-right and up-and-down sequencing. Examples of rebus charts that use sequencing are the charts shown in the companion book for Blob Painting, Mixing Paint, and Vegetable Printing.

REMEMBER: *Do not display rebus charts without the proper introduction and explanation. Children do need assistance from an adult in this initial phase of usage. Periodic reminders will also be necessary.*

HOW TO MAKE REBUS CHARTS

To be educationally correct and used successfully, rebus charts must follow a consistent format. Format guidelines are shown in the following checklist.

✓ Are charts *always* drawn in a *left-right* and *top-bottom* sequence?
✓ Are the drawings representative of the equipment *actually* being used by the children? (It is confusing to the children if the drawings or the steps depicted are even *slightly* different from the ones used in the classroom. It is *important* to adapt the MAKEMASTER® patterns in the companion book to fit your situation.)
✓ Did you check to see if the drawings clearly depict the steps in the process? (Cover the words and look at *only* the pictures and drawings. Try to do the process.)
✓ Is the printing in the manuscript style which is used by the public schools in the area?
✓ Did you add color to the charts with felt-tip markers?
✓ Can you laminate the charts or cover the charts with clear adhesive vinyl?

The patterns for rebus charts included in the companion volume provide basic symbols and drawings for producing many different types of rebus charts. These charts can be the basis for independent-oriented activities for young children. You can use them as shown or as ideas to create original charts for your classroom. Some activities require more adult supervision than others. The amount of supervision will depend upon the individual class. Of course, the safety of the children must be a prime consideration. If an electrical appliance or anything hot is being used, you will want to be there to assist. Suggestions and precautions are included with all the cooking activities and science-discovery experiments in Book 2.

Try out some of the rebus charts. Permit the children to use them in a manner as self-directed as possible. Observe the results. The classroom should have a more independent, self-directed atmosphere with the added bonus of a great deal of indirect learning. The teacher will have to determine the limits and make sure the children follow them. Children learn what they are permitted to do, what is acceptable, and what cannot be done. Adults must help them learn.

REMEMBER: *It will take awhile for teachers and children to adjust to this new and different type of classroom where indirect guidance, self-direction, and independent learning are encouraged within an orderly environment and within predetermined limits. Teachers are interactors rather than supervisors, and children become independent learners.*

General Guidelines for Construction of Charts

This section will discuss general guidelines which are appropriate for all the various types of indirect guidance materials.

Begin With the Proper Equipment and Supplies

Before using any of the suggested patterns for projects, locate a work area that will provide adequate light and space for the project. Clear a table or another flat surface to allow materials to be spread out. A cluttered work area often leads to spills, stray marks, and generally unsatisfactory results.

Gather your construction supplies into a box such as an inexpensive household caddy like the one illustrated. This type of container is usually available in the housewares department of a variety or discount store. The compartments are ideal for the supplies you will need.

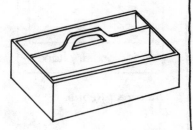

A household caddy helps to organize materials.

The following list of supplies is recommended for the projects contained in this book.

- *a yard or meter stick or metal retractable rule*
- *a one-foot ruler*
- *water soluble felt-tip markers in the eight basic colors*
  These marker tips are approximately ¼″ wide and make broad marks for drawing and lettering.
- *a black nylon-tip pen or marker*
- *oil-base (permanent) felt-tip markers in basic colors*
- *sharpened No. 2 pencils*
- *an art gum eraser*
  These erasers completely remove pencil marks without smudging or smearing the work surface.

- *good quality scissors*
  Invest in a pair of comfortably sized scissors just for paper cutting. Dull scissors can result in jagged, torn edges which can ruin an otherwise beautiful project. If possible, use a paper cutter for cutting the sheets of poster board. If there is not access to a paper cutter, then take time to draw lightly penciled guidelines before cutting with scissors.
- *rubber cement*
  Rubber cement spreads evenly and leaves fewer glue ridges.
- *a utility knife or case cutter*
  The utility knife is a cutting device with interchangeable blades. The case cutter uses razor blades.

Other supplies are project-specific. They include the following:

- *poster board or railroad board*
  These are two common names for medium-weight paper board with one or both sides finished. It can be purchased anywhere school supplies are sold and it comes in assorted colors. The sheets are approximately 22″ x 28″.
- *tagboard*
  This is a lightweight paper board available in 9″ x 12″ and 18″ x 24″ sizes. It is also sold in a variety of colors, as well as manila and white. The major disadvantage to tagboard is that it is too lightweight to stand erect; it must be taped to the wall or table to have the necessary support.

Wash and dry hands

Incorrect Rebus

Specific Guidelines for Rebus Charts

There are a number of considerations for making rebus charts or other pictorial aids to use with young children. One *major* consideration is that pictures in the rebus charts must be "readable" without words. Although the charts will probably contain some printed words or numerals, these printed symbols are for the benefit of the teacher and the few children who are beginning to recognize numbers and letters. The pictures must completely depict the actions for the children. This illustration is an example of an "incorrect" and a "correct" rebus.

1. Wash hands

2. Dry hands

Correct Rebus

A second important aspect is the execution of the printing. Even though the printed symbols are of secondary importance, it is vital that the quality and style of the manuscript, often referred to as printing, be carefully considered and even more carefully executed. The following principles are good guidelines for manuscript printing.

- Always use the manuscript (not cursive) style of printing.
- Be consistent in the style of the manuscript. Make letters the same way each time. For example, use a , not a , a , or A . Varieties of letter styles can be confusing to young children. Select the manuscript style used in local public schools. A pattern for the most common style of manuscript is reproduced in the companion book and is shown here.
- Note that the upper-case letters are a full line or space high, and most lower-case letters are only a half-space high. The lower-case *t* is the only letter that is three-fourths of a space in height. The lower-case *b, d, f, h, k,* and *l* are a full space high. The lower-case *g, j, p, q,* and *y* are the only letters which extend below the main body of the letter.

Alphabet and Numerals for Manuscript Printing

- The first letter of a single-word caption or the first letter of the first word of a phrase is capitalized. The remaining letters are printed in lower-case letters. This style of capitalization is the accepted standard for textbooks and readers. Adoption of this form permits beginning readers to see the printed word as they do when they read.
- Use the manuscript style of printing in all materials used in the classroom, even for any adult bulletin boards. It is important that the parents be familiar with manuscript style so they can reinforce its use at home. It is the best way to ensure that the manuscript will be accurate and neat.

Display and Storage of Charts

Numerous ideas have been presented as "starters" in making rebuses and charts to use with young children. The way they are constructed and displayed and the convenience of storage will determine their effectiveness and usefulness in your classroom. The following suggestions will help you tailor the display and storage of rebus charts to your own situation.

A basic rule for any display method is that the steps or symbols should always be displayed in a left-to-right "reading" sequence or order. Top-to-bottom sequence can be used later.

Begin by taping up to three symbols on the table or tray where they will be used. (See the illustration.) Attach the symbols to the trays with circles of masking tape. It is difficult for young children to change their eye focus from one area to another. Therefore, it is best to place the signs and materials on one plane. The children will have the symbols readily at hand, and the cards can be easily referred to as often as necessary. If possible, laminate the cards or cover them with clear vinyl.

Use tape or pushpins to attach individual cards or small charts to the wall. Chalkboards or easels can support larger charts. They can also be tacked to a bulletin board or hung from pegboard hooks if they are prepunched at the top of the chart.

Table Arrangement

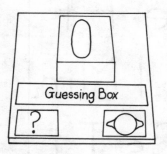

Tray Arrangement

Introduce rebus charts or symbols on a single plane.

Vinyl window shades are effective display devices. If the windows are located directly over the table or shelf to be used, the shade can be lowered, and the charts or cards can be taped to the shade.

Slot charts have been used in many classrooms. They can be purchased at a school-supply store or can be made from heavy cardboard. The slots are cut from poster board and stapled or taped at the sides and bottom. The cards or charts for display are merely slipped into the horizontal slots.

An individual holder for small charts can be made from a plastic spray-can lid, clothespins, and plaster. Mix the plaster and pour it into a lid. Before it hardens, insert a wooden slip-on type clothespin with the open end up. If a pinch-type clothespin is used, wrap a rubber band around the ends so that the clothespin is held slightly open; then insert the clothespin and rubber band into the plaster. After the plaster hardens, place small charts into the slot of the clothespin. Use two holders for larger charts or for two-step directions.

A free-standing triangular display board can be made from three sides of a heavy cardboard box. This display aid can be made in any size and can have several slots for left-to-right and top-to-bottom sequencing of charts, or it can be one long, narrow easel-type display board. First, select an appropriate box. Then cut out three sections that are divided by the corner creases or crease a section with the edge of a knife. Fold the cardboard on the creases to form a triangular shape. Fasten it together with a staple gun or strong tape. Then tape or staple tagboard strips to the box at the desired intervals. In addition to acting as a display board for rebus charts, this box will serve as a roof in the block corner or a table easel in art.

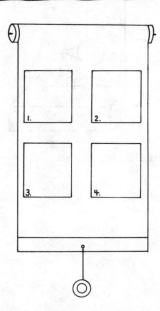

A Window-Shade Rebus Display

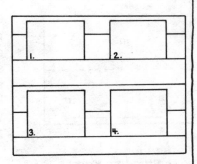

A Slot-Chart Rebus Display

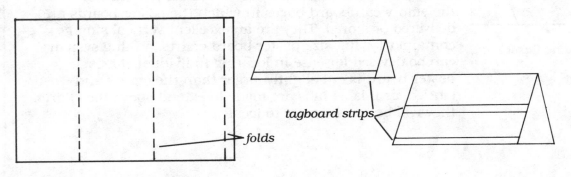

tagboard strips

folds

A Triangular Rebus Display Board

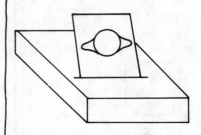

A Box Display Stand

A box can be covered with attractive vinyl adhesive to make a display stand. Cut a slit along the top surface of the box. Then insert the charts into the slot for display purposes. When you are designing the rebus charts remember to leave extra space at the bottom to prevent any part of the chart from being obscured.

A "flip chart" makes a convenient rebus chart display. To make one, design all of the rebus charts to be the same size. Then punch holes along the top edge and thread metal rings, heavy cord, or leather strips through the holes to make a "flip chart" of rebus sequences. Flip charts can be placed over a painting easel and moved around the room.

Egg cartons which are cut into sections and turned upside down can be used to hold small lightweight charts on the table top. The charts can be slipped into the indentations between the sections. Children like to paint them.

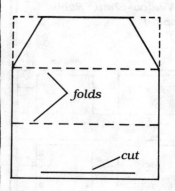

folds

cut

**Pattern for a
Free-Standing Easel**

You can make small easels for single symbols or for short sequences of directions. These triangular stands can be easily stored unfolded. Three small easel holders can be made from one sheet of poster board. Determine the size and carefully cut it out. Then trim one end to form a tab as shown in the illustration. Place a slot in the other end of the strip near the edge. Then crease the poster board by lightly running the edge of a knife at desired intervals for folds. When the chart is creased and folded, the tab can be inserted into the slot to form a free-standing easel.

Store the Charts Creatively

Storage is a major problem for any teacher. The solution is often as creative as the rebus charts.

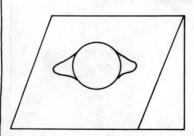

A Free-Standing Easel

Some of the rebus charts can be enlarged and mounted on a full sheet of poster board that can be stored in an upright vertical file. A school supply store will sometimes give away the empty cardboard boxes in which the poster boards are delivered or stored. They are an excellent vertical storage container for full-size poster board charts. A filing system can be devised for ease in locating individual charts. If poster board is cut slightly larger than the charts and labeled, or if label tabs are made to extend above the charts, they will be much easier to locate.

Consider making a "rebus book" for each subject category. Punch three holes in the side of each chart and use metal ring "hinges" so that new pages can be added as charts are made. The children enjoy looking through a book of charts, and it is readily available for their use. The "rebus books" can reinforce classification concepts while providing a convenient storage place.

Another suggestion for storage is to make the individual steps of the rebuses on separate 8½" x 11" pieces of poster board. If the pieces of the charts are made to fit into file folders, they can be readily stored in a box or file drawer. Many different pictorial charts can be stored in a small space. This method of storage affords easy organization and location of charts and keeps them in good condition.

The individual cards can be taped together in a hinged series as illustrated below. This series could be folded for storage and expanded for use with the children. If each series of rebuses is made the same or of a similar size, they could be stored on the book shelf.

Some steps reoccur frequently in pictorial directions, such as washing and drying hands, or hanging pictures to dry. These steps could use the same cards repeatedly in different rebus direction sequences. This system of using individual cards for each step allows drawings that are used frequently to be filed together and to be used over and over again, thereby reducing the number of drawings needed. If you have the companion MAKEMASTER® book, you can photocopy these general-purpose drawings and use them for several rebus activities.

Label each rebus card on the back to indicate the title of the rebus or symbol chart and the number of that step in the sequence. The rebuses cannot be numbered on the front because the numbers will differ. If desired, temporary numbers can be added on the front to reinforce numerical sequence with the children. When using the same steps in several rebus charts, use the same color of cardboard.

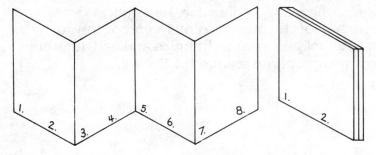

Tape "hinges" can keep rebus cards in order.

5 | *Types of Interest Centers*

In a program stressing self-direction and indirect guidance, interest centers are probably the most useful areas of the room. The interest-center approach is a very effective way to teach young children, resulting in a program which moves smoothly and helps children to think and work for themselves and in cooperation with others. As a teacher, you will have time to interact and give individualized attention.

The room arrangement suggested for an early childhood classroom makes use of interest centers. Interest centers are defined as the areas of the classroom designated primarily for particular activities, interests, and learning. The use of interest centers is an excellent way to facilitate self-directed learning. The particular centers available in any classroom vary with each individual program. Nine possible centers are suggested. A classroom would probably not have all of these centers open at one time. The names of the interest centers discussed in this chapter are the following:

- Art or Arts and Crafts Center
- Library Center
- Blocks or Construction Center
- Dramatic Play Center
- Cooking Center
- Discovery Center (nature/science/math)
- Music/Motor/Movement Center
- Table Games Center (manipulative materials/math/readiness)
- Rotating Centers (for example, Workshop, Water Play)

This chapter offers suggestions for the physical implementation of the interest center concept in your classroom. Actual guidance techniques and activities are discussed in appropriate sections of Book 2.

THE ART CENTER

The Art Center should be near a source of water. The floor should be a smooth material that is easily cleaned. Tables are necessary for finger painting, collage, clay, and other projects. Provide a shelf area for storage and a display area for art projects. The display area can be in the room, in the hall, and even on the ceiling. Easels should be available. They can be a commercial variety or can be made from three sections of a large cardboard box. The display easel described in Chapter 4 can be adapted to make a table easel. Add tape or notches for clip clothespins to attach the paper to the easel. Place a box next to or under the easel to hold paper.

Consider taking art activities outside. Almost everything done inside can also be done outside in good weather. Art lends itself very well to the outdoors, with a fence or a wall providing an ideal painting surface. Small tables and easels can be taken outside. (See Chapter 10, Using Outdoor Interest Centers.)

Ideas for Self-Direction and Indirect Guidance

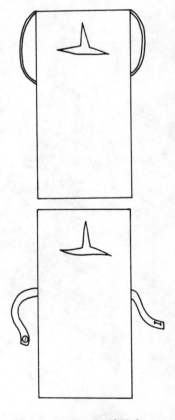

- Make an art mobile or interest-center marker to indicate the Art Center.
- Use simple symbols and rebus charts for activities and use open/closed signs to indicate if the Art Center is available for use. (See Book 2.)
- Use cues or indicators on shelves to show children where items belong. Cue individual trays or boxes of materials for particular activities, such as finger painting.
- Provide self-help smocks. These smocks can easily be made from an old hand towel or flannel-backed material. Cut a slit for the neck. Add a small vertical slit to the neck opening so the smock will go over the child's head. Bind the opening. Add elastic arm pieces or a strip that will wrap around the child's waist to fasten in front with a button, snap, velcro, or a tie.
- Provide rebus charts for art projects. Book 2 includes MAKEMASTER® patterns for the following:

  1. Make Playdough
  2. Finger Painting
  3. Mixing Paint
  4. Easel Painting
  5. Cleaning Paint Brushes
  6. Blob Painting
  7. Vegetable Printing
  8. Collage

Patterns For Self-Help Smocks

- Place the rebus charts in a convenient location so that the children will be responsible for cleaning brushes, mixing paint, and washing tables.
- Arrange display devices for art rebus charts (Chapter 4).
- Provide self-help art supplies such as the following:
  1. A box for easel paper near or under the easels
  2. Trays of cued art supplies that are easily managed by children
  3. Clip-type clothespins or strips of tape for holding paper on easels; or prepunched paper to fit over nails on easels
  4. A drying rack on which paintings can be draped to dry, or a newspaper-lined drying space on the floor
- Try some of the Art Center activities for which rebus charts are provided. The companion book (Book 2) gives teaching suggestions for each of the activities shown in the rebus charts.

When indirect guidance ideas are employed, the Art Center will no longer require a great deal of supervision. It can be an area where the teacher is an interactor rather than a supervisor, and where the children do almost everything in a self-directed way.

THE LIBRARY CENTER

The Library Center is sometimes called the language or story corner. Locate this area in the quietest part of the room. Provide a rack or shelf for books and pictures.

Ideas for Self-Direction and Indirect Guidance

- Make a mobile or Library Center marker. Consider making a "dropped ceiling" or a wall hanging to represent a library.
- Add some symbols to indicate "look," "listen," or "do."
- Include a rocking chair, some pillows, and a "hide-away" to encourage quiet activities. The "hide-away" could be a cardboard refrigerator box with doors and windows cut into it, an easel with a lightweight blanket over it, or a card table with a sheet over it.
- If possible, provide a cued tape recorder or record player with headsets for listening to recorded stories or music. Place a green piece of tape on the "go" lever and a red piece on the "stop" lever and use arrows to point out the direction of movement for volume control.

- Encourage storytelling and language development with puppets and a puppet theater or a flannel board and flannel-board figures. The puppets can be made or can be commercial. Use a commercial puppet theater or make one from a box, table, bookcase, or blocks.
- Develop a picture file for the children's use. Choose favorite pictures from magazines or other publications. Mount the pictures on cardboard. Laminate them or cover them with adhesive-backed vinyl. Store the pictures in a box that is covered with colorful paper, and make dividers from colored cardboard. The pictures can be classified according to categories and color-cued to the cardboard dividers by the color of the mounting material. Picture categories might include animals, children, food, toys, or vehicles. The children will learn filing and classification skills as they get a picture from the file, talk about it, put it up for display, and then return it to its proper location.
- Add shelf markers to indicate the placement of materials.
- Make an "object guessing box" to stimulate language. This is a closed box that contains various objects that can be felt but not seen. The box can be made by cutting a hole in a closed shoebox. Another idea is to place several small objects in a can. Then put the can inside a sock. In either case, the children reach in to feel and guess the contents. Change the objects frequently.
- Make a rebus chart or sign that suggests how to treat books. This rebus could include the suggestion to wash hands and it could show children how to return books to a shelf.
- Place new materials in the library area as various topics are introduced. Permit the children to use them as independently as possible.

THE BLOCK CENTER

Block play is probably one of the most beneficial play activities in an early childhood classroom. The Block Center is an active, noisy place, so locate it near other active areas. If the Block Center is adjacent to the Dramatic Play Center, interaction can occur between them. Since blocks require a lot of space, the Block Center may be in the area set aside for large-group experiences. Consider a smooth-surfaced rug in this area to reduce noise and to facilitate floor play.

Ideas for Self-Direction and Indirect Guidance

- Make a Block Center marker or mobile to indicate the center.
- Use the open/closed sign and simple symbol charts for activities.
- Use cues or shelf indicators to show children the location for different-sized blocks and block accessories. Start with cues that are the same size and shape as the blocks and boxes. When the children understand these cues, use smaller cues that will suggest the relative sizes and shapes. In the beginning, the shapes should be on the same plane as the blocks. Later they can be moved to the back rise of the shelf unit as shown.
- For older children, use different-sized dots or other shapes to indicate different-sized hollow blocks or accessories. For example, the largest hollow block may be represented by a large dot, the middle-sized blocks by a smaller dot, and the smallest blocks by the smallest dot.
- Display pictures to indicate activities or topics being discussed, for example, pictures of buses or trains if the topic is transportation.
- Use a rebus chart to suggest block storage to older children.
- Store blocks on open shelves rather than in a box to encourage self-direction in cleanup.
- Block play is very popular in many early childhood classrooms, so two separate areas are recommended as an ideal arrangement. One of the areas can be located near the Dramatic Play Center and the other on the far side of the block storage area. This arrangement allows two separate groups of children to play at the same time.
- Set up related activities in the Block Center and Dramatic Play Center some of the time. For example, arrange a dressing room in the Dramatic Play Center and a theater in the Block Center.
- Provide for non-sexist education by encouraging girls and boys to play in the Block Center.
- Have convenient storage for extra blocks and accessories.

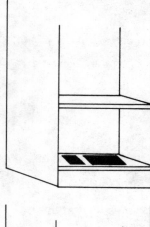

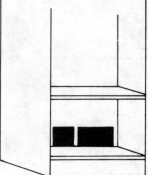

An outline cue can be attached to the floor of a shelf and later moved to the rise of the shelf.

THE DRAMATIC PLAY CENTER

The Dramatic Play Center is the area of the room where housekeeping equipment is located. This area serves a versatile role. As the areas of emphasis in the program are changed, this area changes. It might become a home, a restaurant, a flower shop, or a photography studio.

Ideas for Self-Direction and Indirect Guidance

- Make an appropriate mobile or Dramatic Play Center marker to correspond with the topic.
- Display pictures and symbols to indicate the activities.
- Coordinate activities with the Block Center in order to encourage complementary use of both areas.
- Encourage imagination by making a variety of materials and costumes available. For example, suggest a laundromat by placing a basket of clothes and some pictures of clothes or laundry in the area, but let the children themselves decide to make the toy kitchen sink into a "washing machine" and the toy stove into a "dryer."
- Outline dishes and utensils on paper lining to cue the shelves so that the items can be returned to their places.
- Outline clothing on a pegboard to suggest where to hang dress-up clothes or the clothes for "sale" in the clothing store. Outlines of pots and pans would suggest where these might hang in the kitchen or in a "restaurant."
- Use pictures or unusual boxes to store materials for individual situations. For example, restaurant materials might be stored in a gallon ice cream carton covered with a placemat or menu. An airline's timetable might be used to cover a box of travel things.
- Cue prop boxes according to the items they contain. A box containing hats might be cued with a sketch of several hats. A box of "versatile vests" might be cued with magazine pictures of community helpers such as an office worker, doctor, pilot, bus driver, or a teacher. A box of aprons might be cued with pictures of a baker, a gardener, a cook, a waiter, a florist, or a carpenter. The apron or vest trims correspond to the various occupations. You can easily make some of these versatile vests and aprons from a small piece of doubled fabric (16" to 18") or from the leg of a discarded pair of slacks or trousers. Follow these steps to make the vests:
  1. Cut off the slacks at the knee. Open both side seams on one leg. Then do the same on the other leg. Lay one thickness of fabric on the other.
  2. Retain the hem of the slacks for the hem of the vest.
  3. Cut out a neckline and armholes as shown in the illustration. Sew side and shoulder seams.
  4. Turn under and sew the cut edge to make a facing for fasteners.
  5. Add buttons and button holes, snaps, gripper snaps, a zipper, velcro, or ties.
  6. Add pockets and trim as desired.

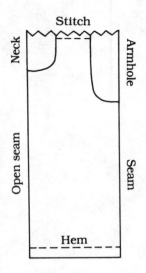

Pattern for a Versatile Vest

Make versatile vests from slacks or from two thicknesses of fabric.

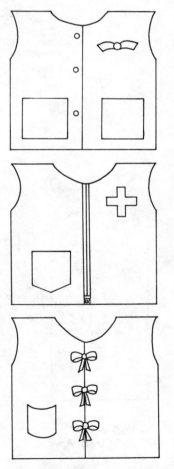

Three Types of Versatile Vests

- Child-sized aprons are useful for dress-up clothes, art aprons or cooking aprons. Follow these steps to make the aprons:
  1. Cut off the slacks at the knees. Cut armholes as shown in the apron illustration, retaining the hem for the hem of the apron. Add a piece of elastic at the neckline so it will stretch over the children's heads and adjust to a variety of sizes. Two aprons can be made from one pair of slacks.
  2. Add a wrap-around tie that will close in the front with a button, gripper snap, snap, or velcro.
  3. Use fabric from the other pant leg for pockets and optional trim to correspond with an occupation.
- Book 2 includes a rebus for Putting Clothes Away. Make rebus charts for other household activities, such as the following:
  1. Washing or scraping dishes
  2. Shaving with an electric or safety razor (cord and blade removed)
  3. Bathing a baby doll
- Bring in a large box and a barrel. Observe how the children use them in dramatic play without suggestions from adults. When the children offer a constructive suggestion, develop a dramatic play activity to go along with it.

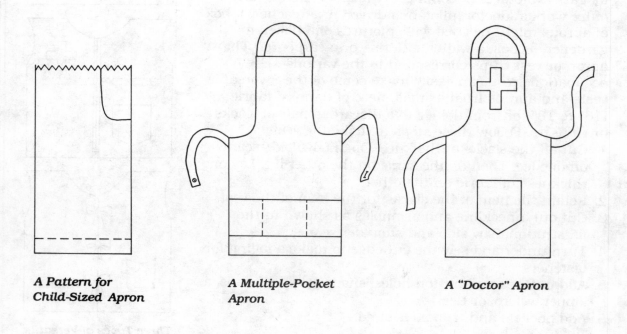

A Pattern for Child-Sized Apron

A Multiple-Pocket Apron

A "Doctor" Apron

THE COOKING CENTER

Cooking may be done as a learning or interest-center activity or as a group experience. Young children benefit more from a cooking experience if the group is small and if each child has a chance to participate. To obtain the best results from a cooking project, allow each child to take part in the whole preparation process. However, there are some cooking experiences that lend themselves to prior demonstration. In this case, you might show the children the process, but give the children the opportunity to follow the rebus and do the activity on their own. Book 2 provides sample rebus recipes and teaching suggestions.

Safety is an important factor in cooking. Any time a hot item, an electrical appliance, or sharp utensils are used, an adult must be in the area to ensure safe use of the materials. The adults do not have to directly supervise, but they must be present.

Ideas for Self-Direction and Indirect Guidance

- Make a Cooking Center marker or mobile to put up on the days when a cooking project will be done.
- When cooking is planned, display the hand-washing rebus and the rebus that tells the children to put on a smock. Remind them to follow the instructions on the rebus.
- Begin with simple cooking projects and advance to more complicated ones. It is meaningful for children in a full-day program to make items from the school lunch menu. Children in a half-day program can make snack items.
- Plan the activities so that all the children get an opportunity to participate if they desire. Different groups of children may participate at various times.
- Outline each cooking utensil on a chart or pegboard and hang the items so the children can get them and return them to their place.
- Draw cuing outlines of materials on tray liners so that they can be returned to the trays.
- Mark cups and bowls to indicate quantities.
- Use graduated cups for measuring dry ingredients.
- Premeasure ingredients for beginning cooks. Later the children may measure from a full container.
- Emphasize nutrition when planning cooking activities. Young children learn to eat a variety of foods if they are exposed to them without prejudice.

1
Put on a smock.

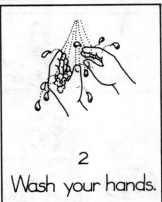

2
Wash your hands.

- Teach children to use sugar and salt in moderation. Snacks do not have to be sweet. Include fresh vegetables as snack items.
- Make a rebus chart of the utensils, equipment, and food products needed for each recipe. Each of the rebus chart patterns in the companion book begins with a rebus of the ingredients that will be needed. Be sure to include this step. It is important to teach children to gather all the materials before beginning.
- Begin with simple cooking rebus charts. Enlarge rebus drawings to show one step to an 8½" x 11" page. Advance to more complex rebus charts as the children become more experienced. Then use two or more rebus drawings to an 8½" x 11" page, with the drawings ordered in sequence.
- Use *realistic* drawings of the ingredients, processes, and utensils that indicate items to be used in the recipe.
- Try some of the cooking recipes for which rebus charts are provided in Book 2. These recipes include teacher suggestions, safety precautions, concepts to emphasize, and related activities. Use them as samples to create your own recipes.
- Use encouragement and praise as the children learn to follow the rebus charts. The children will enjoy the process, learn quickly, and eagerly anticipate days when cooking is available.
- Make a picture-and-word menu to go along with the recipes to help the children make associations between words and names of foods.

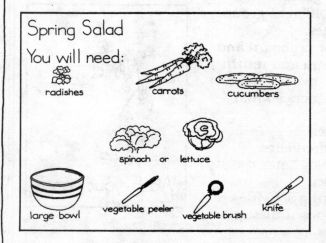

"You Will Need" Rebus Chart

Rebus Chart with Steps

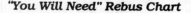

THE DISCOVERY CENTER
(Math/Science/Nature Activities)

This is the area where the children are encouraged to touch, to feel, and to experiment. It is the area of discovery. At one time, this area was called the nature area, but now it is much more. This center is the place for scientific inquiry and the use of the scientific method. Encourage the children to test things, to investigate them, and to figure out new ways to use them. Book 2 provides rebus charts and teaching suggestions for activities appropriate for this center.

A caged small animal, some plants, and a few shells might be located here. Encourage the children to bring things from home and to display them on a shelf. Make a low table available for experimentation, for manipulation of materials, and for displaying the things to be discovered.

Ideas for Self-Direction and Indirect Guidance

- Make a mobile or Discovery Center marker for the area.
- Display pictures and symbols relating to discovering things and to nature, science, measuring, weighing, and comparing.
- Display a large question-mark symbol to encourage the children to think or question. Add an eye and a hand symbol to suggest that they look, touch, and do.
- Include many testing or investigative activities where the children have to predict what will happen, try an activity, and check their prediction. Make rebus charts explaining the experiments. The rebus chart activities shown in the Discovery Center section of Book 2 are Bubble Blowing, Absorption, Color Mixing, Float or Sink, Will It Attract, and Water Mixing.
- Use the "open/closed" and "yes/no" symbols in the center.
- Provide cued box lids or trays to hold materials.
- Have some egg cartons, ice cube trays, or other divided containers for classification activities.
- Provide a low table with comfortable chairs.
- Place magnets, magnifying glasses, prisms, scales, rulers, and other science- and math-related items on a cued shelf in the Discovery Center. Decorate a storage box with a space theme or other science-related theme.
- If a caged animal is in the class, print the animal's name and a story about it on the cage. The story can be dictated by the children and recorded in manuscript printing. Then the children can illustrate the story. They will recognize the words when they see the illustrations.

THE MUSIC/MOTOR/MOVEMENT CENTER

Music and movement can be combined in a learning or interest center, as well as in a group experience. Locate this center near the Block Center in a noisier area of the room. The center could also be in the group-experience area with a piano, a record player, and/or tape recorder. Tone bells, an autoharp, rhythm instruments, scarves, and other movement props will encourage rhythms and movement.

Ideas for Self-Direction and Indirect Guidance

- Make a Music/Motor/Movement Center marker or mobile. Use pictures and symbols that refer to music and movement. Some cutouts of musical notes and a music staff mounted on a large piece of fabric or cardboard suggest the music concept to the children.
- Cue the storage of musical instruments and movement props by drawing their outlines on a screen or bulletin board. Then add hooks at each outline so that children can hang the instruments.
- Cue the piano to indicate notes and songs that have been similarly cued. (See Chapter 3 for specific directions.) Children can learn to play simple tunes.
- Try the rebus chart activities provided in the Music/Motor/Movement section of Book 2.

TABLE GAME CENTER

This area of the room is sometimes called the manipulative center because puzzles, shape boxes, visual-motor toys, games, and similar floor- or table-type toys are located in this area. Sometimes this area is called a readiness center because of the many preacademic activities planned here.

Ideas for Self-Direction and Indirect Guidance

- Make a mobile or Table Game Center marker.
- Use pictures and action symbols to indicate activities.
- Place materials on the shelves to correspond with the concepts that are being taught. Provide a convenient place to store other items. Don't overload the shelves. The children become confused by too much.
- Include some rug squares if the floor is not carpeted. Many toys, such as building sets, suggest floor games.

- Provide tables for most manipulative-type toys, especially puzzles and board games.
- Cue instructions to the games with rebuses whenever possible. This will encourage self-direction.
- Ask questions that encourage children to put their knowledge to work. Ask "Why?" "How?" "What do you think might happen?" and "What else can you think of to do with that?"
- Cue the game storage by drawing outlines around games and table toys on the shelves so that the children know where to return them.
- Include games that involve finding same and different forms, and classification of objects. MAKEMASTER® patterns for "same or different" are found in the companion volume.
- Make or purchase some tray games and trays or containers. If all the items necessary for the activity are on a tray, it becomes a vehicle for indirect guidance. The children select a game from the shelf, place it on a tray, use it on the tray, and return everything to the proper place on the shelf. Lids or baskets can also be used to contain the games.
- Include several object boxes or guessing boxes. The box may be a surprise box (described with the Library Center), or it may be an open box. The child retrieves an object from the box and interacts with it in some way. It may be played with, discussed, or matched one-to-one with a symbol or a representation of that symbol. For example, a lid might be matched to another lid or it might be matched to a symbol that represents all metal things. Rebus charts can be made for this matching activity. The correct responses can be placed on the reverse side. In this way, the children can check their answers themselves.

These kinds of toys teach children to function independently. The teachers offer suggestions and ask questions, but children know that they can use the toys as the cues indicate. You may join the children to observe and to help them move to higher levels of cognitive learning.

THE ROTATING CENTERS

Some interest centers may appear occasionally according to the activities being encouraged, the needs of the children, the topic being studied, or the weather conditions. These centers may be indoors or outdoors. If you have a large classroom, you might plan a space for a rotating center or "surprise center."

For example, the Cooking Center can be a rotating center if it is not used every day. Water play can be a rotating center activity, as can the workshop. You might add a balance beam or a gym mat to the Block Center to make it more useful on a rainy day.

The Dramatic Play Center can be a rotating center as it is changed from a "kitchen" to an "airliner" to a "bakery shop," or it can reflect a topic being discussed or a study trip. The children might suggest new arrangements during a time when the class is talking about a topic such as the zoo or a circus.

The Library Center can become a puppet theater, a movie theater, or a place to see plays. It is a good idea to maintain part of the library area as a quiet area.

Rotating centers can be tailored to meet the individual needs of the program. Variety will maintain the children's interest and will provide for added activities in the classroom.

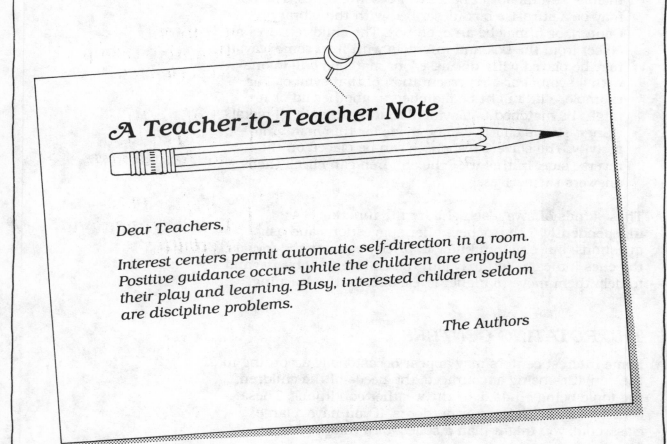

A Teacher-to-Teacher Note

Dear Teachers,

Interest centers permit automatic self-direction in a room. Positive guidance occurs while the children are enjoying their play and learning. Busy, interested children seldom are discipline problems.

The Authors

PART II

Indirect Guidance Through Activities

 Chapter 6
Scheduling

 Chapter 7
Establishing Routines

 Chapter 8
Setting Limits

 Chapter 9
Planning Group Experiences

 Chapter 10
Using Outdoor Interest Centers

 Chapter 11
Using Transitional Activities

6 | *Scheduling*

A good schedule is the framework for effective indirect guidance in the classroom. The schedule guides the interplay of group time, individual time, and daily routines. It balances the needs for quiet time and active play and teaches young children what is expected of them. As the children learn the sequence of the daily tasks, you will be free to interact with them for learning rather than for management purposes.

Where good indirect guidance techniques are used in an early childhood program, young children will often verbalize the schedule. "First we have a snack, next we wash up, and then we sing songs." This feedback indicates that the teacher has appropriately used routine scheduling of activities as an effective indirect-guidance technique.

Staff members should carefully plan the schedule before school starts. All responsible adults are then aware of their responsibilities during each part of the program.

During the first few weeks of school, the schedule should be followed very carefully. Once the routine is firmly established, changes can be made without upsetting the children. Simple explanations will be necessary. For example, on a day that threatens rain, the teacher may say, "Today, we are going outside *first*, because it looks like it might rain. We might not be able to go outside later. There will be time for indoor play before lunch." This simple explanation lets the children know the reason for the change. It also reassures them that they are not going to miss an activity they might be anticipating.

USING A SCHEDULE

In planning a self-directive class, it is extremely important to use indirect guidance techniques in the schedule. These techniques are inherent in each of the following factors for developing a preschool schedule.

Routines

Carefully plan routines, such as arrival and departure, mealtimes, rest, and toileting. Effective use of routine time is important to the smooth operation of a preschool class. Indirect guidance ideas to use during routines are developed in Chapter 7.

Space and Time Requirements

When making your schedule, consider the space and time requirements of other classes using the same facility. Coordination of each class schedule is important. Combine children of various age groups if it is compatible with your program and if such combinations adhere to state licensing standards. Plan to minimize overstimulation when scheduling combinations of age groups. If children arrive and leave on a staggered basis, groups can be successfully combined at the beginning and end of the day. Quiet, self-directive activities work well for these times.

Balanced Activities

Active Time vs. Quiet Time.   Alternate active and quiet times in the schedule. Children need periods to calm down and rest after an active time. For example, a story time can follow outdoor play. Outdoor stories under a tree or in a quiet corner can be very relaxing. Plan a place in the room where some children can get away to help them calm down on their own. A refrigerator-box house; a sheet thrown over an easel to make a tent; or a quiet area with a rocking chair, some pillows, and a tape recorder with tapes might all provide such a place.

From time to time it might be necessary to remind the children to calm down. To do this indirectly, suggest an interesting quiet activity. An alert teacher will anticipate when a particular child or a group of children needs quiet time.

Group Time vs. Interest-Center Time.   The alternate scheduling of group time and interest-center time will provide children with variety and help them to tolerate constraints. Participation in an organized group activity for any length of time is extremely difficult for preschool children. Group time should be short and have as few pressures as possible. Group time should be followed by periods which are less structured, such as time in an interest center or some outdoor play.

Allow sufficient time for interest-center activities so that all children have an opportunity to complete projects. Also, give yourself time to interact with individuals and groups of children. Some children require a long time to be actively involved in one area, while other children will take part in several activities during one interest-center period. Make provision for both groups of children. It is usually recommended that children *not* be required to switch centers, as it is very frustrating. The children should not be forced to stay in a center once they have completed an activity. However, there should be enough time for complete involvement in the activity. Ideas for indirect guidance in interest centers are included in Book 2.

Large-Group Time vs. Small-Group Time. Plan some large-group activities that involve all or most of the children. However, these times should take into consideration the age and attention span of the children. Plan these periods well so that all children will have an opportunity to participate without spending a great deal of time waiting for a turn.

Scheduled time in small groups is extremely important for young children. If most group activities are planned for small groups, children have more opportunities to participate, and they receive more individualized teaching.

Transitional Activities

Transitional activities help children move from one activity to another. They usually take the form of fingerplays, songs, requests, or other activities that are either direct or indirect. Chapter 11 gives ideas for transitional activities using indirect-guidance techniques.

Staff Availability

When planning a schedule, take into account the needs and availability of staff members at various times during the day. Staff–child ratios must be maintained in an early-childhood program. Volunteers can often contribute significantly. There should be time to plan, to attend meetings, and to be away from the classroom for awhile. Planning staff schedules is an important part of developing a schedule for an early childhood class. The goal is the efficient use of all available resources.

A SAMPLE SCHEDULE

Develop a schedule to meet the needs of the children, school, and staff. The following schedule is included as a reference. Each program is unique and its planning is an individualized process.

SAMPLE SCHEDULE FOR A CLASS OF PRESCHOOLERS*

7:30 a.m.—Arrival of Children; Greeting by Caregiver; Self-selected Activities

8:15 a.m.—Cleanup; Transitional Activity

8:30 a.m.—Group Time; Language Activities; Music

9:00 a.m.—Restroom; Breakfast-type Snack; Socialization at Table

9:15 a.m.—Group Time; Concept Activity; Plans for Day

9:30 a.m.—Interest/Learning Center Activities (Art, Table Games, Blocks, Dramatic Play, Library, Readiness Center, Music, Cooking, Discovery [science], Workshop)

10:30 a.m.—Cleanup Time; Transitional Activities; Group Time (Music, Movement, Story Time) and/or Directed Learning Activities

11:00 a.m.—Outdoor Activities

11:45 a.m.—Cleanup; Transitional Activity; Restroom (Children in half-day program depart)

12:00 p.m.—Lunch; Socialization at Tables (Self-service)

12:30 p.m.—Restroom; Brush teeth; Quiet Transitional Activity to Rest Time

1:00 p.m.—Rest; Quiet Activity and/or Individualized Activities

2:00 p.m.—Music; Motor/Movement Activities

2:30 p.m.—Interest/Learning Centers and/or Small Group Activities

3:15 p.m.—Cleanup; Restroom; Snack; Socialization at Tables

3:30 p.m.—Language Activities; Story Time; Sharing Time

4:00 p.m.—Outdoor Play (Groups may be combined if there is a staggered departure.)

4:30 p.m.—Cleanup; Departure

*Adapted for half-day program.

A Teacher-to-Teacher Note

Dear Teachers,

Remember that each class is different. Every schedule will vary. The end goal should always be kept in mind; that is, the schedule should create a quality program for young children—one that develops independent learners who are self-directed and self-disciplined.

The Authors

Establishing Routines

Routines are a necessary part of the daily schedule in any early childhood program. In a classroom that encourages self-directed activities, routines can be utilized as teachable moments. Sometimes the classroom routines can provide an environment for parent communication. The routines that lend themselves to indirect guidance techniques are the following:

- arrival and departure
- eating (snacks and meals)
- sleeping and resting
- toileting
- grooming

As part of the daily schedule, self-directed activities are used to help the children learn to do and enjoy routine tasks.

MAKING USE OF ARRIVAL AND DEPARTURE TIMES

Arrival and departure times offer an opportunity to encourage self-direction in the children and to communicate with their parents.

Provide a place near the door for the children to keep their belongings and to store things to take home. Each child needs his or her own space, marked with the printed name and his or her special symbol. Mark each coat hook in the same way. If a place is provided for their coats and other things, the children will indirectly learn orderliness and will be more responsible for their belongings.

Many parents like to be aware of classroom activities. Arrival and departure times are often their only contact with the classroom. As you implement these suggestions for parent communication, remember that parents are often in a hurry and are sometimes uncomfortable about leaving their children for extended periods of time. Contacts with parents should be brief, but friendly. In many cases, indirect communication ideas work best because parents can read the messages without waiting to speak with the teacher. The following are a few successful ideas.

A "Topic of the Week" Poster

- Make a "Topic of the Week" sign that has a pocket for parent handouts. Many parents like to reinforce school activities at home, and young children frequently are not good about telling what has been done. The handouts can include songs, fingerplays, stories, reports of trips, and notes about other classroom activities.
- Post a "Where Did You Play?" chart near the entry door. Print the names of the interest centers horizontally across the top. List the children's names down the side. Each day the teacher or the children indicate where each child has played. Add a new page to the chart each week so that it is a cumulative record.
- Post a lunch or snack menu, notices of coming events, stories, and art projects. These items all help bring the school activities home to the parents.
- A "What We Need" poster, like the one shown below, is interesting to the parents and helpful to teachers who use a lot of "junk" items. Attach samples of the actual items that will be used in projects so that the parents know what to save. Clearly mark the date when you will need the materials. Then place a box or basket under the poster to receive the contributed objects.

LEARNING TO SOCIALIZE AT EATING TIMES

Snack or mealtimes provide many opportunities for indirect guidance. The children need to learn that mealtime is a time for socializing and practicing social skills. This is a time for the practical application of many other learned behaviors,

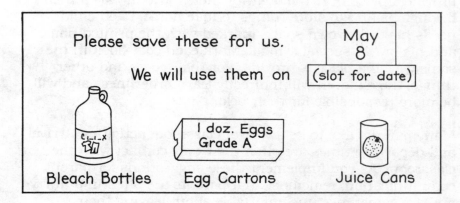

A "What We Need" Poster

such as taking turns and cleaning up after oneself. The children will particularly enjoy eating food that they have prepared using the rebus charts.

Consider these ideas for self-direction and indirect guidance.

- Make placemats that show accurate indications of where items belong. For example, trace around a plate, a glass, and utensils.
- Use a seating chart to assign seats at the tables in order to encourage some eating pattern or habits. Directed learnings might be given to children who are having difficulty with social skills or who have poor appetites.
- Reserve this time to teach some special skill indirectly. For example, mealtime conversation may be in a second language, especially if many of the children know or frequently hear that language. Also, mealtimes may offer an opportunity to indirectly teach sign language.
- Post a weekly menu that includes pictures of the foods that will be eaten each day.
- Some classrooms use a "Helpers Chart" in conjunction with eating and other routines. The board shows the names of the children who are the helpers for the day. Jobs might include setting the tables, scraping the plates, wiping the tables, or sweeping the floor. Early in the year the children decide what the helpers will do. Each job is assigned a number. Then each child makes an outline of his or her handprint on cardboard or heavy paper (or use the MAKEMASTER® handprint pattern). Print the children's names on the handprints and punch a small hole near the top. Then store the handprints in a set of "Yes" and "No" pockets at the bottom of the chart. The handprints for children who have completed their jobs are stored in the "No" pocket. Place hooks on the chart to correspond to each job. Choose helpers for the day and place their name handprints on the appropriate hook. Place the numbers of the jobs on the back of the handprint so that everyone can keep track of which jobs the children have done.

A Placemat Rebus

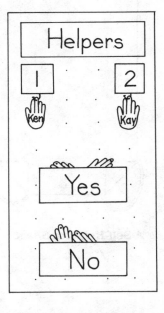

A "Helpers Chart"

ENCOURAGING SELF-HELP AT REST TIMES

A rest or sleep time is part of most early childhood programs. Frequently, children have difficulty settling down for this period. Some of the children really require a rest, while others need only to have time to calm down. If the children participate in scheduling this time, they will accept it more readily.

You can use the self-directive teaching approach by permitting the children to help decide on the length of time for rest or nap time. Offer acceptable choices that fit into the requirements of the program and any state licensing standards. With indirect guidance, the children can decide which times they wish to rest on their cots or mats, how long they should look at books or play quietly, and how and what they should do when those times are up. Quiet activities and directed learning experiences can be available for children who have rested the specified time.

Self-help cot sheets are another indirect guidance technique for rest times. Changing the cot sheets can provide a self-directed learning experience if the sheets are made correctly. Cut the fabric to fit the cot measurements plus two inches on each side to provide for 1″ double hems. Turn over the corners at a right angle and stitch them down. Sew elastic to the outer corners of the triangles formed at two corners. The children fasten the other two ends with strips of fabric which can be snapped, buttoned, or tied. Mark cots with each child's name and symbol and provide a cot chart that tells where the child's cot is located.

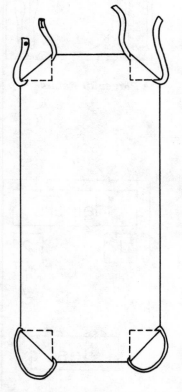

A Self-Help Cot Sheet

Children's artwork can be displayed from the ceiling and walls in the rest area. Children's cots can be placed under their art. When the children see their art, they will know where to find their cot or mat. The artwork provides something to focus on while resting but not sleeping.

USING INDIRECT GUIDANCE AT GROOMING TIME

Rebus charts are very effective indirect guidance techniques for grooming time. A rebus for washing and drying hands will remind the children to do this from the beginning of the year. The children will remember to wash, rinse, and dry their hands and to throw the paper towel in the trash. Other rebus charts that work well for grooming are those for brushing teeth, toileting, and using tissues. If flossing is part of the routine, a rebus can be made for it. Teach the proper brushing technique, and, more important, the technique of flossing. Very young children can learn to floss. If the child has a toothbrush, it should be marked with the child's name and symbol. Disposable styrofoam cups marked with names and symbols can be used to store toothbrushes. Floss can be easily stored in the dispenser.

Setting Limits

As teachers of young children, we are responsible for meeting their physical and emotional needs. These needs include food, sleep, clothing, exercise, and fresh air. Children also need to know that they are needed and accepted; that they are loved and wanted; and that someone cares and approves of them and what they do.

In the same way, children need and want guidelines and limits for controls and guidance. Through their participation in setting limits, young children understand the classroom guidelines and tend to claim ownership of those guidelines. The limits also allow the children to be more self-directed within the parameters established for the classroom. Knowing what is expected of them, the children feel secure.

Some of the factors to consider in setting limits are:

- understanding the need for limits
- planning for individual differences
- deciding on limits
- setting the limits
- enforcing the limits

UNDERSTANDING THE NEED FOR LIMITS

Without limits, children are not sure where they stand and how much they can do. Children need limits. Yet, too many or unrealistic limits cause children to become frustrated.

Realistic limits help children to identify the boundaries within which they are expected to function and help them to regulate their lives. Limits offer security. They define what is acceptable during periods of development when children are not able or ready to do certain things on their own. In addition, limits assist children in moving from a current level of learning to a higher level in an acceptable fashion. Finally, limits let children know that someone cares enough to be concerned about what they do.

PLANNING FOR INDIVIDUAL DIFFERENCES

Teaching situations vary and each group of children has its own characteristics. Consequently, consideration must be given to these variables when setting limits. The following list includes some typical areas to be considered.

- stages of maturation and development
- ages of the children
- degree of necessity for limits
- unusual circumstances
- consideration of the rights of other children and adults
- consideration for personal property
- health and safety factors
- relationship of the limits to the activity or the situation

DECIDING ON LIMITS

Some limits are "teacher-made rules" which are a part of the classroom procedure. They are established at the beginning of school and are inherent in the arrangement of the classroom, the schedule, and the routines to be followed. When matter-of-fact reminders from children and teachers are given in a positive way, these rules are accepted as part of the classroom situation. This type of limit might include walking instead of running in the classroom and cleaning up after oneself.

Other rules are situation-specific. When these behaviors are within the children's power to control, the rules should be made with the children's help. If children make the rules, they tend to accept them. The children feel responsible for the rules. The responsibility is removed from the teacher and placed on the children. Since the children must adhere to the rules, they should be the ones responsible for them insofar as they are ready and able.

When considering involving the children in setting limits, ask yourself these questions.

- Can the children really make these particular rules or limits?
- Can I accept or "live" with the children's decision?

If you decide to involve the children in setting limits, view the results in the light of these questions.

- Are the limits reasonable?
- Are the limits realistic?
- Are the limits simple?
- Are they stated in a positive way?
- Can they be written in a simplified manner?

INVOLVING THE CHILDREN

Consider the desired results of involving children in setting limits. The goal is a cooperative, relaxed, self-directed classroom situation where indirect teaching and learning can occur. An equally important goal is to encourage socially responsible children who respect the rules and can make a worthwhile contribution.

The limits must be fair, reasonable, and realistic, no matter who makes them. Children are sometimes much harder on themselves when making rules than adults are. When children make the rules, adults must help them see what is realistic, reasonable, and real. These are abstract concepts and understanding them will be a very slow process.

Whenever possible, permit the children to set the limits with an understanding adult who will allow the children to express their ideas, but who can lead them along lines that will be acceptable to the children and the adults who use the classroom. In general, the group of children who are making the limits should be no larger than five. Four or five young children can successfully work together in this rather organized task. Permit each child in the group to have a voice in the decisions. Listen to all the points of view. One child cannot be permitted to dominate.

Limit the number of rules made with the children to no more than five at one time. They should tell what *is* to be done, not what *is not* to be done. Finally, the children should understand that they are responsible for carrying out the rules with the assistance of understanding adults.

Write the rules down on a large tablet using manuscript printing. Use pictures or drawings to illustrate the rules. When agreement has been reached, go over the limits with the other children, again in small groups. Ask them if they have any additional rules to add. If they do, add them.

ENFORCING THE LIMITS

The most important part of any limit-making situation is carrying out the letter and spirit of the rules. Limits are effective only if they are enforced. You will need follow-through and reminders, although many children do a very good job of helping each other abide by the rules that they have helped to formulate. Consider these guidelines.

- The children should be responsible for helping to honor and enforce the limits. Reminders will be necessary.
- Allow the children to think through the consequences of not following the rules. This will be easier if they can verbalize the rules. Anything that can be said can be put into written form. Children also learn that what is written down has a great deal of meaning. When the children cannot remember or verbalize a rule, they can show where it is by using the illustration on the written rules, and the rule can be read together. This process reemphasizes the importance of writing.
- Whenever possible, give choices between acceptable alternatives. If there is no choice, do not permit one. If the answer is "no," do not offer a "maybe."
- Be consistent in enforcing the limits. However, under certain circumstances, a situation may warrant "looking the other way" and not calling group attention to the error.
- Recognize the children's feelings. Give them a chance to think through the situation and reconsider. Instead of stating the rule for them, permit them to recall the rule. For example, when they come into the room, ask them, "What do we do first when we come in?" This is a way to remind them to hang up their coats instead of throwing them on the floor.
- Leave an "out" for the children to help them save face or to give them another chance. For example, you can ask, "Do you want to try that again?" Another way is to say, "I'm sure you'll remember next time. For now, let's go sit and think about it."
- When a child "tests" the limits, be firm but friendly, staying within the rules that have been decided upon. Giving in will cause many children to test the limits even further the next time.
- Always make sure the limits are fair, realistic, and reasonable.
- Do not become emotionally involved when enforcing limits. State the rule or have the child state it. Show the child the rule on the list and expect conformity.

- Give positive attention to the children who have difficulty with the limits. If they can succeed at something, they will be more responsive. Try to make sure that children leave for the day feeling good about themselves as people.

AN EXAMPLE OF SETTING LIMITS

The following example will help to clarify how the use of limits can work in a classroom where self-direction and indirect guidance techniques are used.

Ms. Brown generally had a calm, relaxed class. She was a low-keyed teacher who enjoyed young children. Her classroom included interest centers and she and Mr. Sandy, the team teacher, employed indirect guidance techniques. A routine had been established and the schedule was understood by most of the children. However, two weeks had gone by, and things were not going as she would have liked. There was much hitting and tattling among certain children.

Mr. Sandy and Ms. Brown decided that five children were having a particularly difficult time, and that Mr. Sandy would have a "talking time" with these five to see if something could be done. Mr. Sandy asked the children to stay in one afternoon to do something very special with him. He did a fingerplay with the children and ended up laughing with them. Then he told them he had something else he would like to discuss with them. He honestly stated the problem and asked the children if they had any solution.

Max and Billy immediately started discussing the hitting at length. Mr. Sandy suggested that he print "Hitting" on the big tablet as a problem. Maria and Robert mentioned the fact that other children always knocked their buildings over.

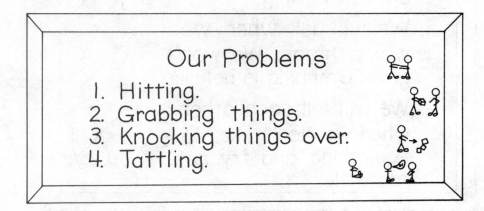

Our Problems
1. Hitting.
2. Grabbing things.
3. Knocking things over.
4. Tattling.

They said it made them angry when someone grabbed things from them. Mr. Sandy did not place the blame on anyone, but he did acknowledge that knocking things over and grabbing were problems. Marie started talking about tattling. She said that Patty always ran to Ms. Brown and told. Mr. Sandy suggested that he write down and illustrate their problems.

Mr. Sandy then asked if they had any suggestions about what they could do. They started making all kinds of suggestions. Mr. Sandy listened awhile and then said, "May we put those down in some rules? Let's begin with hitting." He suggested a positive statement about telling the child instead of hitting. The children insisted that the rule should state that they would not hit. He wrote that down. Then Mr. Sandy helped them verbalize some more rules and added the pictures. Their final rules statement looked like the illustration below.

Mr. Sandy said, "I think these are good rules. Let's read them together." Mr. Sandy read the rules with them. Then he suggested that they tell the other children the rules when they returned from recess. Then they all went out to play.

Our Rules

1. We will tell someone when we don't like something. We will not hit.

2. We will only knock down our own things.

3. We will ask when we want things. We won't grab. Grabbing is not nice.

4. We will tell each other when we don't like something and try not to tattle.

What happened?

- The children who were involved made the rules.
- The rules were simple.
- The teacher offered suggestions but listened to the children's ideas and wrote them down.
- The rules were realistic and reasonable.
- They dealt with the problems directly.
- The children were given the responsibility of helping to share the rules with the other children.

This example shows a positive way to establish limits. The children who were misbehaving were involved, so the chances are that they would be more likely to remember the rules and would help the other children remember too. The goal of self-direction was reinforced through an indirect guidance approach.

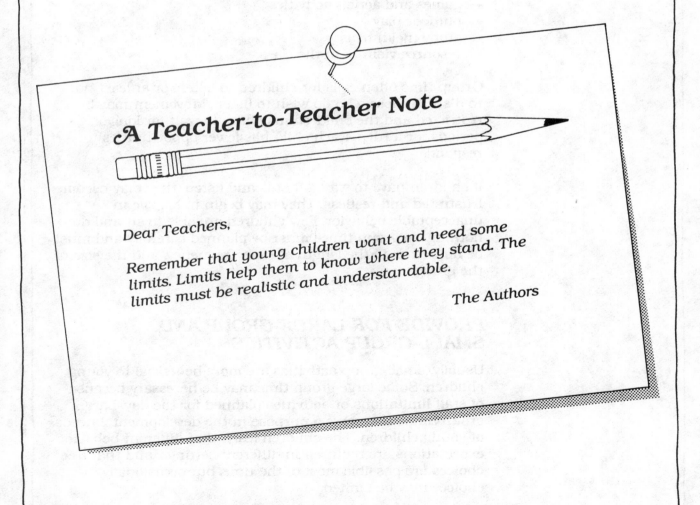

A Teacher-to-Teacher Note

Dear Teachers,

Remember that young children want and need some limits. Limits help them to know where they stand. The limits must be realistic and understandable.

The Authors

9 Planning Group Experiences

Group experiences are those activities that children do with other children in the class. These experiences might include the following:

- gathering times to start or end the day
- planning and evaluation time
- sharing time or show-and-tell time
- music and movement activities
- motor or physical education type activities
- story or language arts activities
- games and action activities
- outdoor play
- study (field) trips
- resource visitors in the class

Group time often calls for children to listen, or at least not to disturb those who do wish to listen. Movement may be restricted and the children may have to wait for longer periods for a turn. Each child has fewer opportunities to respond.

If children have to wait, sit still, and listen, they may become frustrated and restless. They may begin to engage in unacceptable behavior. Few children are able to sit and do nothing, so group times must be planned carefully and must be limited as to the length of time, frequency, and the size of the group.

PROVIDE FOR LARGE-GROUP AND SMALL-GROUP ACTIVITIES

Usually, small-group activities are more beneficial to young children. Some large-group time may be necessary because of staff limitations or activities planned for the day. Large-group times also serve a purpose in the developmental needs of young children. The children learn that different behavior expectations are required in different settings, and that free choices are possible most of the time, but occasionally choices may be limited.

Three-year-old children can usually spend 10 to 15 minutes in a group activity with a group of no more than 12 or 15 children if provisions are made for some movement. Four-year-olds can manage 15 or 20 minutes of large-group activities, and five-year-olds may be able to stay with a group activity for as long as 30 minutes. It is extremely important to schedule alternate quiet and active times and times for interest-center activities.

Small-group activities are extremely important for young children. A group of 6 to 8 children offers the opportunity for much more individual attention and feedback from the teacher and the other children. A good rule to follow is, "The smaller the children, the smaller the group."

Make an area of the room available for a large-group gathering. At least one, but preferably two or three small-group areas, should be available. A teacher does not have to be present with each group. In a class where self-direction and independent learning occurs, children can conduct their own group activities. At times, you may have to get the group started on a story, a musical activity, or a share time, but you can move on to another group, feeling that the children will manage. Leaders sometimes emerge, or the children work together as a group.

USE INDIRECT GUIDANCE FOR GROUPS

Some ideas for indirect guidance in large- and small-group experiences include:

Grouping with Symbols

Group children by using a symbol for each group. It may be the cutout of an animal or a colored piece of paper in the shape of a circle or a triangle. Corresponding indicators are also placed in each of the group areas and given to the children. The small indicators may be distributed as a transitional activity (see Chapter 11). For example, the area indicators might be yellow circles, red squares, and blue triangles. The individual indicators might be smaller versions of the same shapes.

Grouping by Area

Another way to group the children is to designate particular areas, for example, the circle area, the triangle area, and the square area. (Colors, objects, or pictures could be used.) A mobile could mark each area. The children's nametags would reflect an area's shape or color. The children could match their nametag designs with the corresponding area marker. The advantage of this method is that the children have a stable group and really get to know the other children in their group. The grouping process is very simple and smooth. You can change nametag symbols periodically in order to obtain changes in groupings.

Communicating with Symbols

During group time, use the basic eye, hand, ear, and nose symbols that are discussed in Chapter 4. The symbols can be used to gain attention, to give directions, and to provide variety. Hold up one or more of these symbols to indicate an action indirectly. An *eye* and a *mouth* tells the children to look and then talk. A *question mark* and a *hand with an international slash through it* tells the children to think but don't touch. The guessing-game quality is a motivating factor for the children, and they are responding to indirect clues.

Using Signing

Other symbols are also effective in teaching the children a new idea without verbal involvement. Young children can easily learn some simple hand moves used in sign language. It is easy to learn the signs for the actions "see," "go," and "come" and the words "yes," "no," and "pretty." The children enjoy this new and different method of communicating. A visit from a person who does signing is also a worthwhile learning experience. Tell the visitor the signs that the children know, so that they can communicate.

Using Charts

Teach group movement and music skills using rebus charts. The charts included in Book 2 are:

1. Beanbag Toss
2. Elastic Circles
3. Movement Bag
4. Rhythm Instruments

Making An Obstacle Course

Use hand and footprint patterns to make a circular obstacle course for a group experience. Hand and footprint patterns are shown in the companion MAKEMASTER® volume. Teaching suggestions are provided in Chapter 10 of this book.

Using Musical Symbols

Use the patterns for the musical symbols in the companion volume for clapping out rhythms, playing instruments, or doing guessing games. Most of these activities are much more beneficial if done in small groups of five or less.

Blowing Bubbles Outdoors

Create a group experience with the Bubble Blowing rebus for a group activity of blowing bubbles. This can be done inside but works particularly well outdoors. (See the Bubble Blowing rebus in Book 2.)

Sharing Songs and Stories

Use rebus stories and songs during small- or large-group story or music time. "Hush, Little Baby" is a sample of a rebus song. Many other songs could be adapted for use with rebus charts. Commercial rebus stories could be drawn larger on a large flip-type kindergarten tablet and then used for group story time. Try to limit the size of the group to five or six children. When more children are involved, it is difficult for the children to see.

Employing Transitional Activities

Use transitional activities to teach groups of children in an indirect way. The songs, fingerplays, and action activities discussed in Chapter 11, Using Transitional Activities, will offer many indirect, smooth, and efficient ways of moving children from one activity to another.

Cooking as a Group Activity

The cooking recipes in Book 2 lend themselves to small- and large-group experiences. They can also be done in interest centers. Each rebus recipe includes suggestions for using that recipe. The size of a cooking group should be small so that all children have a chance to participate. Cooking activities can be done several times in one day, on successive days, or, if the teacher keeps a record of who participates, over an extended period. In this way all the children have an opportunity to participate.

Whether in a large group or a small group, indirect guidance techniques can be employed in a self-directed classroom where the teachers are interested in providing times for the children to discover on their own. These children become independent thinkers with a minimal amount of adult intervention.

In a self-directed early childhood setting where indirect guidance is used, the outdoor environment is extremely important. The children need and like to be outside. Outdoor periods permit children to relax and to release tension. Fewer constraints are placed on the children outdoors than in most other parts of the program.

The teacher with outdoor duty must recognize the responsibilities of the job. Interaction, questioning, offering suggestions, and encouraging the children are all part of outdoor responsibilities. The teacher can offer more spontaneous activities outside. Children need time to develop play situations on their own. However, a teacher can place materials outside for the children to use in their play situations. This will result in constructive and appropriate play times.

Almost anything that can be done inside can also be done outside. Tables, chairs, blankets, blocks, easels, and almost anything else can go outside if the weather permits. Even in rainy weather, small groups of children can enjoy the outdoors. A walk in the rain with three or four children in raingear is an excellent way to discover some of the wonders of nature.

PLAN A MOTOR/MOVEMENT CENTER

The outdoor area is an excellent place to develop motor and movement skills. Riding tricycles, climbing, jumping, crawling through tunnels, playing with a parachute, and playing with large playground balls are naturals for motor development. However, you can make this area an interest center for motor and movement skills by using the ideas for indirect guidance provided in the Music/Motor/Movement section of Book 2. These activities include the Beanbag Toss, Elastic Circles, and the Movement Bag.

Children Playing With A Parachute

SET UP AN OBSTACLE COURSE

An obstacle course is an excellent activity to provide self-directed learning. These courses can be cued by using the footprint and handprint symbols from the companion book. Arrange some tires in a circular or snake-like pattern. The children will step or jump in and out of them. Add an oil-barrel tunnel to crawl through, a walking beam or balance board to balance on, and a ball to bounce in and out of a tire or box. Draw hand- or footprints with chalk between the parts of the obstacle course.

If you set up the obstacle course so that it goes in a circle, there will be no beginning or end. Ask the children to help in setting up the first one. Draw a diagram of the course on a piece of poster board and put it up outside. The next time, see if the children will arrange the course themselves. Encourage changes and draw a new diagram for the course, letting the children tell you the changes.

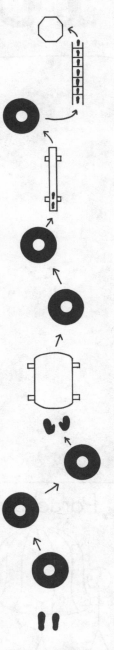

A Straight Obstacle Course

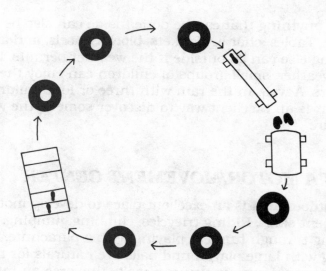

A Circular Obstacle Course

Obstacle courses can teach many concepts. Courses that use chairs and tables can suggest to the children that they go *under, around, behind, next to, in,* and *out.* Reinforce these spatial words as you interact with the children. Temporal words, such as *first, next,* and *last* can also be introduced and reinforced. Motor development, language development, and cognitive development are all reinforced by this type of activity.

PLAN AN OUTDOOR ART CENTER

Art activities lend themselves to an outdoor setting. Easels and tables can be brought outdoors. All the activities suggested by the patterns in the Art Center section of the companion book can be done outside. Set up the art materials outdoors and place the rebus charts on an easel or on one of the display devices discussed in Chapter 4.

Other art activities suggested by the outdoors include making a nature collage, painting with paint brushes and food coloring, making a mural on the fence, and box art, using large cardboard boxes. Make a space for a mural by tacking a large piece of poster board or butcher paper to the fence. Then let the children paint it. A cloth mural can also be done outside. Hang an old sheet from the fence and let the children paint it with paint or water-base marking pens. You can go over their artwork with a permanent marking pen to make it permanent. (The permanent pens are toxic.) This type of artwork makes an excellent tablecloth for picnics or a drop ceiling for the classroom.

OFFER DRAMATIC PLAY OUTDOORS

Outdoor dramatic play is varied. Some situations are more natural when they are acted outdoors. Consider these dramatic situations.

- a box "space ship," "rocket," or "satellite"
- a box "train," "bus," "car," or "airplane"
- a garden, garden shop, plant nursery, or flower shop
- an "ice cream cart," "lemonade stand," or "snow-cone concession"
- a circus or a zoo

Provide the necessary props. Include a collection of large and small boxes and let the children create with them.

PROVIDE AN OUTDOOR CONSTRUCTION CENTER

Self-directed block play is more convenient outdoors. Shipping boxes make excellent blocks. Boxes can be stuffed with newspapers and sealed with masking tape, or the boxes can be used as they are and discarded as they break. Provide and mark a corner of the play yard for them and expect the children to return them to their corner. Bring block accessories from the classroom. If there is an outdoor storage facility that is weatherproof, hollow blocks can be left outdoors. If not, or if they are to be used both inside and outside, the blocks can be stored near the exit door so that each child could bring one outside as he or she exits.

ENCOURAGE DISCOVERY AND SCIENCE OUTDOORS

The science experiment charts can all be used outdoors as successfully as inside the classroom. Put up the appropriate rebus in an outdoor area. Add a table and the experiment tray.

Encourage outdoor gardening, looking for insects, studying plants and weeds, nature walks, and child-originated discovering.

PLAN A QUIET CENTER OUTDOORS

Bring library books, puppets, and table games outdoors. Place a table in a corner of the playground or under a tree. Rug squares or a blanket provide an excellent place to read a story or interact with puppets. "Show-and-tell," spontaneous conversations, and sharing can occur. A quiet time after outdoor play is a calming activity. The children all gather together to share ideas and to evaluate the day before going in for lunch or leaving for the day.

EXPERIMENT WITH AN OUTDOOR MUSIC CENTER

If an outdoor electric outlet or a heavy-duty extension cord is available, you might bring a record player or a tape recorder outdoors. However, it is not necessary to have music to do musical activities. You can play musical games by chanting the words. The outdoors provides more room for active musical games such as "London Bridge" and "Here We Go Round the Mulberry Bush." You can begin these games, inviting the children to join in if they so desire. Musical instruments can be brought outdoors. Try to make outdoor activities spontaneous.

OFFER WATER/SAND/MUD PLAY OUTDOORS

Water play is a relaxing activity for children. It can be done indoors or outdoors. A water table is a good addition to a classroom, but several dishpans will suffice. An interest-center marker could signal the days when water play will be available outside so the children are aware that it will be there. A mobile is a good outdoor indicator for water play. Hang it from the roof if it will withstand the weather. The mobile might be made with a child's beach pail as the base. Suspend a bubble pipe, a plastic bottle, a funnel, or other water-play toys.

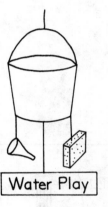

A Water-Play Mobile

Water-play toys can reinforce the concepts of measuring, full/empty, and sameness. Include graduated cups and different size containers with graduated markings. Have child-size sponges and brooms available for cleanup. When water play is inside, provide small mops and sponges. The children can wear smocks made from old towels, or, in warm weather, they could wear swimming suits or "cutoffs."

Permit the children to use sand, cornmeal, oatmeal, beans, or sawdust as a medium in the water table. Ask questions which will encourage the children to think about the activity and the materials. Questions should begin with "Why?" or "How?" to require thinking.

In warm weather, suggest that the children bring swim suits to school. Young children enjoy a wading pool, running through a hose spray, or mud play.

SET UP AN OUTDOOR WORKSHOP CENTER

Because a workshop center is noisy, it is ideally located outdoors. In some climates this is possible most of the year. In other areas, it must be a seasonal activity, or the center must be moved indoors during foul weather.

Provide a workbench or a work table for sawing and hammering. Any *old* table will suffice. It is good to have a vise or C-clamps to hold wood while sawing. Provide *real tools*, not toys. The workshop materials can include wood scraps, styrofoam pieces, cardboard, popsicle sticks, tongue depressors, nails, screws, bolts, and glue. Goggles are suggested.

A workshop is a place for many activities. Craft projects, wood sculptures, styrofoam crafts, box art, and toothpick art all lend themselves to the workshop.

For safety reasons, the workshop must be supervised very carefully. However, self-directed activities and some indirect guidance are still possible. Consider the following ideas for workshop techniques.

Teaching Suggestions

- Make a Workshop Center marker to put up in the workshop when it is available.
- Place appropriate pictures and symbols in the classroom to indicate that the workshop is being used.
- Make rebus charts to go with workshop projects.
- Cue a pegboard with outlines of tools.

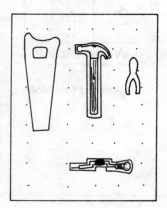

A Pegboard Cued With Outlines of Tools

- Nail cans of different sizes to a board to hold nails of various lengths. A similar container could be used for screws, washers, nuts, bolts, and other items. Consider using an ice cube tray or a sorting tray or box (available in tool departments) to teach classification.
- Cue storage areas with a chart to show the children and adults where workshop tools belong.
- Provide a box of spools and a rebus to show the children how to put a spool over a nail before hammering. This technique will protect children's fingers. (A pinch-type clothespin can also be used to hold the nail while hammering.)
- Drill small holes in a board and start the nails that will be hammered. This step will make hammering easier.
- Presaw wood so that the children will have an easier time when learning to saw. Make a thin saw line and permit the children to complete the cut.
- Give lots of praise and encouragement in workshop endeavors.
- Encourage both girls and boys to use the workshop.

The outdoors provides as much opportunity for learning as does the classroom. Think of the outside as an extension of the indoors. Self-directed activities and indirect guidance are easily encouraged outside.

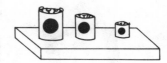

Store Workshop Center nails in cans nailed to a board. Cue the cans to show the various sizes of the nails within.

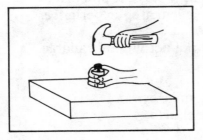 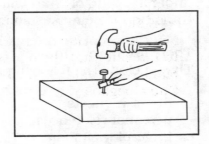

Rebuses For Hammering

A rebus can teach children how to put a spool over a nail before hammering.

A clip-type clothespin can protect little fingers and hold the nail that is to be hammered.

11

Using Transitional Activities

Transitions are changes from one condition, form, stage, or activity to another. In the early childhood program, transitions occur frequently as children go through the day's routine. The ways by which the children move from one activity to another are called *transitional activities.*

Transitional activities are an extremely important part of an early childhood program. The time span between two activities can leave children without direction. These periods include cleanup time, the time before and after group activities, outdoor play, rest time, and any time a change occurs in the routine. Long periods of waiting encourage children to behave inappropriately. Few children are able to sit and do nothing. An unplanned transition time often leads to attempts to over-control the children, sometimes resulting in conflict between teacher and children. You can simplify transition times if the children have a clear understanding of what will be coming next. A smooth transition time makes an enjoyable learning experience.

There are many kinds of transitional activities available. They include the following:

- direct requests
- personal references
- fingerplays, music, or action songs
- signals, symbols, or charts
- props
- cognitive concepts

DIRECT REQUESTS

When a teacher uses direct requests to move the children from one activity to another, a small number of children are told to do something. For example, the children may be told, "It is time to get ready for lunch." These requests to a group of young children are frequently ineffective. Little children respond better if the teacher will go from group to group and tell them, "In five minutes it will be time to clean up and get ready for lunch." The children are then prepared for the transition. Remind them when the five minutes are up.

PERSONAL REFERENCES

Personal references that apply directly to a child are good transitional activities. Children like to have you say their name or say something about them. Even a shy child responds with pleasure when the teacher says, "The person wearing a purple striped shirt may go to the bathroom first. He is _____ ." Of course, the other children will call out the child's name. You might then ask, "Johnny, who would you like to choose to go with you?" Or you might say, "All the children whose name starts with *M* may go outside" or "Children with brown hair may find a place at the table." Other possibilities for personal references include the following:

- "All the children who are wearing tennis shoes may. . . . ."
- "The children who have had their fifth birthday. . . . ."
- "Those children who are wearing jeans may. . . . ."

These personal references are extremely important to young children, who tend to be egocentric and will do something much more willingly if a personal reference is made to them.

FINGERPLAYS, MUSIC, OR ACTION SONGS

The use of fingerplays, musical activities, and action songs is an effective way to quiet children or to get children to move from one activity to another in an indirect manner. These activities are interesting and fun for the children and serve to gain their attention. Fingerplays and action songs tend to quiet the children. To have the children seated and quiet, try one of the following exercises.

RAGDOLL

Flap your arms.
Tap your feet.
Let your hands go free.
Be the raggiest ragdoll
You ever did see.
Now fold your hands
And quiet be.

GRANDMOTHER'S GLASSES

These are Grandma's glasses
This is Grandma's hat.
This is the way she folds her hands
And puts them in her lap.

Here are Grandpa's glasses
Here is Grandpa's hat.
This is the way he folds his arms
And sits like that.

ROLL THEM AND ROLL THEM

Roll them and roll them and give a little clap.
Roll them and roll them and put them in your lap.

TOUCH EXERCISE

I'll touch my hair, my lips, my eyes,
I'll sit up straight, and then I'll rise.
I'll touch my eyes, my nose, my chin,
Then quietly sit down again.

CLAP YOUR HANDS

Clap your hands, clap your hands,
Clap them just like me.
Touch your shoulders, touch your shoulders,
Touch them just like me.

Tap your knees, tap your knees,
Tap them just like me.
Shake your head, shake your head.
Shake it just like me.

Clap your hands, clap your hands,
Now let them quiet be.

TWO LITTLE HANDS

Two little hands go clap, clap, clap.
Two little feet go stomp, stomp, stomp.
One little body turns around.
One little child sits quietly down.

TEN LITTLE FINGERS

I have ten little fingers and they all belong to me.
I can make them do things, Would you like to see?
I can make them jump high. I can make them jump low.
Or I can fold them together and hold them just so.

You do not have to have a good voice in order to use songs
as transitional activities. If the tune is not known, the words
can be chanted or a tune can be improvised. Try some of the
following songs to indirectly suggest activities.

I SEE

I see "Rosa." I see "Gardo."
Please stand up. Please stand up.
Do a little clapping, and a little jumping.
Walk to the door. Walk to the door.

(Change the name, the action and the direction.)

SOMEONE'S WEARING

I see someone wearing blue, wearing blue, wearing blue.
I see someone wearing blue. Who are you?

(Teacher points to a child.)

The child responds, "I am _____ ."
Teacher says, "It's time for you to _____ ."

COME FOLLOW ME

Come follow, follow, follow
Come follow, follow me.
Come follow, follow, follow
And here is where you'll be:
(state place)_____ .

If the same song or fingerplay is repeated to indicate specific activities in the day's schedule, the children will anticipate what is going to happen next. When using these transitional activities, introduce only one new fingerplay or verse at a time to avoid confusion. Repeat the words and action several times. The children will begin to join in after several repetitions. With the younger children, choose songs and fingerplays with only a few words. Participation and movement make the activity more interesting. Fingerplays and songs not only serve as transitional activities, but they aid in fine motor development, teach concepts, and serve as fillers between activities.

Many songbooks and several fingerplay books are available commercially. Teacher friends may have favorites that they are willing to share. Learn a few of them well and use them regularly with the children.

SIGNALS, SYMBOLS, AND CHARTS

A signal can tell children it is time to do a particular thing. Holding up a finger can mean "Listen." A note on the piano or on a musical toy, such as the tone bells or a xylophone, can signal to the children that it is time to clean up or go to a particular activity. You might use a timer to indicate the end of an activity time. (A timer that plays a tune is better than one that buzzes.) A verbal signal may be sung or chanted. For example, you might chant, "Listen! Listen! Listen! It's time to listen now."

These signals tell the children that something is to be done, and after several repetitions they soon learn what the signal means. Then you can omit the verbal explanation. The nonsense signals "Ta-DUM" or "Fiddle-DEE" are fun for some children and can be meaningful signals.

You can signal the children through your body language. If you stop what you are doing, go to the group area, and sit down, usually several children will follow. As the others see the children involved in a fingerplay or an activity with you, they will come, and soon almost all the children will join the group.

If a whistle is used as a signal, it should be used sparingly and cautiously. It is somewhat harsh and should be reserved for outdoor time or for a study trip when it is essential to gather all the children together.

The basic action symbols discussed in Chapter 4, and shown in Book 2 as MAKEMASTER® patterns, can be used successfully for transitions. Holding up an *ear* symbol can indicate listening, an *eye* symbol tells the children to look, and a *question mark* tells them to think. If a negative request is required, the symbol with the international slash can tell the children *not* to do something. A mouth with a slash indicates not to talk and a slash through the hand symbol tells the children not to touch.

If you use two or three action symbols or combine them to make a chart, more information will be given. Arrows or signs can signal which direction to go and can lead the children to a particular area. Footprints leading to a specific location can show the children where to go. A stop sign in an interest center will tell the children that the center is temporarily closed.

You can make charts that include words and pictures which the children can "read." A rebus chart at the door which shows the children going somewhere and the words "Study trip to _____ ." can indicate to the children that it is time to get ready for a study trip. If the children's nametags for a study trip are laid out on a table, the children can be taught to get them, put them on, and return to the rebus chart in preparation for leaving. On the chart, show a picture that is representative of the particular study trip. The destination can be left blank, and the printed words which correspond to the study trip can be put on a strip and taped to the chart or inserted in slots on the chart. (See Chapter 4 for instructions on making a slot chart.)

PROPS AS TRANSITION DEVICES

The use of props will help children move from one activity to another. Showing a special puppet can let children know that it is time to come for a story. They will know it is time to cook if you set out a tray with a mixing bowl and a spoon and put up a cooking rebus. A ball can indicate that it is outdoor time. Placing the study-trip nametags on a table can indicate a study trip, and a record player can tell the children that it is music time. All these props serve to signal the children and to let them know it is time to change activities.

COGNITIVE CONCEPTS

Cognitive concepts are built in to many of the transitional activities. For example, asking all the children who are wearing blue socks or brown shoes to go to the restroom reinforces color identification and serves as a transitional activity. Counting games offer many math readiness ideas. You can move the children indoors by chanting songs such as "One Potato, Two Potato" or "One Little, Two Little Indians" while letting the child who ends the chant enter the classroom first. When doing this chant, the teacher touches one child each time a word is said. When the chant comes to the word *more* in "One Potato" or *boys* in the Indian song, the teacher stops and that child may leave to go to a new activity.

Spatial or temporal relationship exercises can be transitional activities. Ask the children to stand *in back of, next to,* or *in between* as they line up. This activity is much more interesting than merely lining up.

Good transitional activities can accomplish the following:

- stimulate the movement of children
- unify the routine
- change the mood of the activity
- permit orderly movement from one activity to another
- provide for individual expression
- help the children feel good about themselves
- enhance development in language, physical, and cognitive concepts
- give children an opportunity to make choices
- gain attention and interest
- tell the children what to expect

When planning and doing transitional activities, remember these steps.

1. Be sure children understand what is expected of them.
2. Keep the initial activity simple. Slowly increase the complexity as the children understand.
3. Begin with short requests, songs, and fingerplays.
4. Increase the length of the activities as the children become accustomed to the transitions.

As you use indirect techniques to change behaviors and to help young children move from one activity to another, these transitional activities will become a part of the daily routine. You will think of new ways to encourage children to become more self-directed and develop independent work habits.

A Teacher-to-Teacher Note

Dear Teachers,

You have an important role in making program and classroom teaching decisions. Your decisions will help to mold the life attitudes of the children in your care.

As former teachers of young children, and now as teachers of future teachers here at the San Antonio College Child Development Center, we share an interest in indirect guidance techniques and a conviction that the techniques, activities, and physical arrangements that encourage self-direction are beneficial for the children, and for the adults involved in the program as well.

Each of us has seen the need for more self-direction in the classroom. We have observed that teachers in the early childhood classroom were spending up to 75 percent of their time doing management tasks rather than teaching. There was an obvious need for more time and energy to be directed toward individual children and toward specific teaching tasks. When we studied the situation, we found that the classrooms where self-direction was encouraged provided more opportunities for the children's development as well as offered more time for the adults to teach.

If we could choose a few words to share with you as a fellow teacher or caregiver in an early childhood setting, we would strongly urge you to consider the benefits of instituting indirect guidance techniques in your classroom. At first glance, it may seem an overwhelming task to make the rebus charts, arrange the interest centers, cue areas and materials, but please consider the end results of these projects. First, the classroom will be organized for the benefit of you and the children. Second, you will be more free to teach rather than constantly having to direct the children. Third, the children will be learning skills of decision-making, social cooperativeness, and self-direction.

We are convinced that the independent learners and doers of today are the independent thinkers of tomorrow. The desire to share this conviction was the major reason for writing this book. We have shared our collection of principles and ideas with our students and within our professional organizations. Now we wish to share them with you. Please feel free to use this manual and to adapt its ideas for use in your classroom. Good luck!

The Authors

About the Authors

Each of the authors of LET THE KIDS DO IT! is on the faculty of San Antonio College in San Antonio, Texas. Norma Ziegler is an assistant professor in the Child Development Center. Betty Larson is an associate professor in the Child Development Department, and Jane Byers is an assistant professor in the same department.

5691